AMAZING ANIMALS
OF THE WORLD ②

Volume 5

Gull, Great Black-backed — Loach, Stone

GROLIER

First published 2005 by Grolier, an imprint of Scholastic Library Publishing

For information address the publisher: Grolier, Scholastic Library Publishing
90 Old Sherman Turnpike
Danbury, CT 06816

Set ISBN: 0-7172-6112-3; Volume ISBN: 0-7172-6117-4

Printed and bound in the U.S.A.

Library of Congress Cataloging-in-Publications Data:
Amazing animals of the world 2.
p.cm.
Includes indexes.
Contents: v. 1. Adder—Buffalo, Water -- v. 2. Bunting, Corn—Cricket, Bush -- v. 3. Cricket, European Mole—Frog, Agile -- v. 4. Frog, Burrowing Tree—Guenon, Moustached -- v. 5. Gull, Great Black-backed—Loach, Stone -- v. 6. Locust, Migratory—Newt, Crested -- v. 7. Nuthatch, Eurasian—Razor, Pod -- v. 8. Reedbuck, Mountain—Snake, Tentacled -- v. 9. Snakefly—Toad, Surinam -- v. 10. Tortoise, Gopher—Zebu.
ISBN 0-7172-6112-3 (set : alk. paper) -- ISBN 0-7172-6113-1 (v. 1 : alk. paper) -- ISBN 0-7172-6114-X (v. 2 : alk. paper) -- ISBN 0-7172-6115-8 (v. 3 : alk. paper) -- ISBN 0-7172-6116-6 (v. 4 : alk. paper) -- ISBN 0-7172-6117-4 (v. 5 : alk. paper) -- ISBN 0-7172-6118-2 (v. 6 : alk. paper) -- ISBN 0-7172-6119-0 (v. 7 : alk. paper) -- ISBN 0-7172-6120-4 (v. 8 : alk. paper) -- ISBN 0-7172-6121-2 (v. 9 : alk. paper) -- ISBN 0-7172-6122-0 (v. 10 : alk.paper)
1. Animals--Juvenile literature. I. Title: Amazing animals of the world two. II. Grolier (Firm)
QL49.A455 2005
590--dc22

2005040351

About This Set

Amazing Animals of the World 2 brings you pictures of 400 fascinating creatures and important information about how and where they live.

Each page shows just one species—individual type—of animal. They all fall into seven main categories or groups of animals (classes and phylums scientifically) that appear on each page as an icon or picture—amphibians, arthropods, birds, fish, mammals, other invertebrates, and reptiles. Short explanations of what these group names mean, and other terms used commonly in the set, appear on page 4 in the Glossary.

Scientists use all kinds of groupings to help them sort out the thousands of types of animals that exist today and once wandered here (extinct species). Kingdoms, classes, phylums, genus, and species are among the key words here that are also explained in the Glossary (page 4).

Where animals live is important to know as well. Each of the species in this set lives in a particular place in the world, which you can see outlined on the map on each page. And in those locales the animals tend to favor a particular habitat—an environment the animal finds suitable for life, with food, shelter, and safety from predators that might eat it. There they also find ways to coexist with other animals in the area that might eat somewhat different food, use different homes, and so on. Each of the main habitats is named on the page and given an icon/picture to help you envision it. The habitat names are further defined in the Glossary on page 4.

As well as being part of groups like species, animals fall into other categories that help us understand their lives or behavior. You will find these categories in the Glossary on page 4, where you will learn about carnivores, herbivores, and other types of animals.

And there is more information you might want about an animal—its size, diet, where it lives, and how it carries on its species—the way it creates its young. All these facts and more appear in the data boxes at the top of each page.

Finally, you should know that the set is arranged alphabetically by the most common name of the species. That puts most beetles, say, together in a group so you can compare them easily.

But some animals' names are not so common, and they don't appear near others like them. For instance, the chamois is a kind of goat or antelope. To find animals that are similar—or to locate any species—look in the index at the end of each book in the set (pages 45-48). It lists all animals by their various names (you will find the giant South American river turtle under turtle, giant South American river, and also under its other name—arrau). And you will find all birds, fish, and so on gathered under their broader groupings.

Similarly, smaller like groups appear in the set index as well—butterflies include swallowtails and blues, for example.

Table of Contents
Volume 5

Glossary...4

Gull, Great Black-backed...5

Hardun...6

Hare, Arctic..7

Hartebeest..8

Hartebeest, Hunter's (Hirola)....................................9

Hawkmoth, Broad-bordered Bee................................10

Hedgehog, Algerian..11

Heron, Little Blue...12

Heron, Nankeen Night..13

Heron, Purple...14

Hog, Pygmy...15

Hornbill, Red-billed...16

Horntail, Large...17

Horse, Przewalski's..18

Horsefly, Cattle..19

Hyrax, Cape...20

Jacamar, Rufous-tailed...21

Jacana, Wattled..22

Jackal, Black-backed..23

Jellyfish, Trumpet-stalked (Stauromedusan).................24

John Dory, European..25

Katydid, Steppe..26

Kingsnake, Prairie...27

Kudu, Greater..28

Kudu, Lesser..29

Langur, Common...30

Lapwing...31

Lemur, Gentle Gray...32

Lizard, California Legless..33

Lizard, Common Cape Girdled..................................34

Lizard, Italian Wall...35

Lizard, Lyre-headed...36

Lizard, Sand..37

Lizard, Short-horned..38

Lizard, Slender Glass...39

Lizard, Smooth-headed Helmeted.............................40

Lizard, Southern Alligator.......................................41

Lizard, Wall..42

Loach, Coolie...43

Loach, Stone..44

Set Index..45

Glossary

Amphibians—species usually born from eggs in water or wet places, which change (metamorphose) into a land animal. Frogs and salamanders are typical. They breathe through their skin mainly and have no scales.

Arctic and Antarctic—icy, cold, dry areas at the ends of the globe that lack trees but see small plants grown in thawed areas (tundra). Penguins and seals are common inhabitants.

Arthropods—animals with segmented bodies, hard outer skin, and jointed legs, such as spiders and crabs.

Birds—born from eggs, these creatures have wings and often can fly. Eagles, pigeons, and penguins are all birds, though penguins can't fly through the air.

Carnivores—they are animals that eat other animals. Many species do eat each other sometimes, and a few eat dead animals. Lions kill their prey and eat it, while vultures clean up dead bodies of animals.

Cities, Towns, and Farms—places where people live and have built or used the land and share it with many species. Sometimes these animals live in human homes or just nearby.

Class—part or division of a phylum.

Deserts—dry, often warm areas where animals often are more active on cooler nights or near water sources. Owls, scorpions, and jack rabbits are common in American deserts.

Endangered—some animals in this set are marked as endangered because it is possible they will become extinct soon.

Extinct—these species have died out altogether for whatever reason.

Family—part of an order.

Fish—water animals (aquatic) that typically are born from eggs and breathe through gills. Trout and eels are fish, though whales and dolphins are not (they are mammals).

Forests and Mountains—places where evergreen (coniferous) and leaf-shedding (deciduous) trees are common, or that rise in elevation to make cool, separate habitats. **Rainforests are different (see below).**

Fresh Water—lakes, rivers, and the like carry fresh water (unlike Oceans and Shores, where the water is salty). Fish and birds abound, as do insects, frogs, and mammals.

Genus—part of a family.

Grasslands—habitats with few trees and light rainfall. Grasslands often lie between forests and deserts, and they are home to birds, coyotes, antelope, and snakes, as well as many other kinds of animals.

Herbivores—these animals eat mainly plants. Typical are hoofed animals (ungulates) that are common on grasslands, such as antelope or deer. Domestic (nonwild) ones are cows and horses.

Hibernators—species that live in harsh areas with very cold winters slow down their functions then and sort of sleep through the hard times.

Kingdom—the largest division of species. Commonly there are understood to be five kingdoms: animals, plants, fungi, protists, and monerans.

Mammals—these creatures usually bear live young and feed them on milk from the mother. A few lay eggs (monotremes like the platypus) or nurse young in a pouch (marsupials like opossums and kangaroos).

Migrators—some species spend different seasons in different places, moving to where more food, warmth, or safety can be found. Birds often do this, sometimes over long distances, but others types of animals also move seasonally, including fish and mammals.

Oceans and Shores—seawater is salty, often deep, and huge. In it live many fish, invertebrates, and even some mammals, such as whales. On the shore birds and other creatures often gather.

Order—part of a class.

Other Invertebrates—animals that lack backbones or internal skeletons. Many, such as insects and shrimp, have hard outer coverings. Clams and worms are also invertebrates.

Phylum—part of a kingdom.

Rainforests—here huge trees grow among many other plants helped by the warm, wet environment. Thousands of species of animals also live in these rich habitats.

Reptiles—these species have scales, lungs to breathe, and lay eggs or give birth to live young. Dinosaurs are thought to have been reptiles, while today the class includes turtles, snakes, lizards, and crocodiles.

Scientific name—the genus and species name of a creature in Latin. For instance, Canis lupus is the wolf. Scientific names avoid the confusion possible with common names in any one language or across languages.

Species—a group of the same type of living thing. Part of an order.

Subspecies—a variant but quite similar part of a species.

Territorial—many animals mark out and defend a patch of ground as their home area. Birds and mammals may call quite small or quite large spots their territories.

Vertebrates—animals with backbones and skeletons under their skins

Great Black-backed Gull
Larus marinus

Length: 28 to 31 inches
Wingspan: 60 to 66 inches
Diet: various vertebrates and invertebrates; also flesh of dead animals
Number of Eggs: 2 to 3

Home: northern Europe, Iceland, Greenland, and eastern North America
Order: Waders and gull-like birds
Family: Gulls and terns

 Oceans and Shores

 Birds

© LYNDA RICHARDSON / CORBIS

Simply by its hunting behavior, it's easy to tell that the great black-backed gull is a very aggressive bird. It attacks puffins in midair, grabbing its victims by the neck. The gull also snatches birds off the ocean's surface or as they venture out of their nests. Sometimes two gulls will even gang up on prey, working together for their meal. This huge bird, one of the largest gulls in North America, is easily recognized by its large size and its black back, as well as by its assertive behavior.

This gull will eat almost anything! It devours birds, bird eggs, and mollusks, and will even visit garbage dumps to find food. It eats dead animals that have washed ashore and will follow fishing boats to eat the wastes thrown overboard. The black-backed gull is a thief, too, robbing fish from other seabirds.

Although silent while flying and seeking food, black-backed gulls are raucously noisy at their nesting grounds, usually located on rocky coasts. They create quite a racket with their screaming, croaking, and crying. Perhaps most disturbing to people is a sound they make that eerily resembles human laughter. Since these gulls nest in large colonies, the noise can be deafening.

The great black-backed gull lays its eggs during May and June, in large nests. The nests, sometimes more than 15 inches in diameter, are constructed of grasses, seaweeds, and mosses. Both parents incubate the eggs and care for the young.

Hardun
Agama stellio

Length: 12 to 16 inches
Number of Eggs: 3 to 8
Home: Europe, the Middle East, and northern Africa

Diet: mainly insects
Order: Agamids and chameleons
Family: Agamids

 Grasslands

 Reptiles

© HANS REINHARD / BRUCE COLEMAN INC.

The shy hardun is Europe's only agamid lizard. This large family of lizards includes many dramatic species, such as the frilled lizards and flying dragons of Africa and Asia and the frightening moloch of Australia.

The familiar hardun is most often seen perched on stone walls in old vineyards and farms. Although this reclusive lizard has learned to live near humans, it is quick to dive out of sight should anyone approach too closely. The hardun's native home includes the Arabian deserts, the grasslands of southeastern Europe, and several hot, rocky islands in the Aegean Sea.

The male hardun is brightly colored, while females and young are a drab color that helps camouflage them. The brightness of the male may help him to attract a mate. The hardun is known for its flat, broad body and a distinctive triangular head. Its round ear openings are quite visible.

The hardun has an especially efficient way of warming itself in the sun. It crawls up a vertical surface, such as a wall or cliff, and then holds its body at an angle. The angle of the hardun's body is carefully aligned with the angle of the sun's rays. In the early morning, when the sun is low in the sky, the hardun holds itself almost parallel to the ground. Around noontime the lizard stands straight up and down. In this way the hardun is able to absorb the maximum amount of the sun's warming energy.

Arctic Hare
Lepus timidus

Length of the Body: 19 to 28 inches
Length of the Tail: 1½ to 4¼ inches
Diet: weeds, grasses, berries, buds, and bark

Weight: 5½ to 6½ pounds
Number of Young: up to 12
Home: Alaska, Canada, and northern Europe and Asia
Order: Lagomorphs
Family: Rabbits and hares

 Arctic and Anarctic

Mammals

© STEVE AUSTIN / WWI / PETER ARNOLD, INC.

The arctic hare is a large and stocky cousin of the familiar jackrabbit. In North America, arctic hares live only in the northernmost regions of Alaska and Canada. Farther south, they are displaced by the more adaptable snowshoe hare. In Europe and Asia, arctic hares range in northern and central regions.

When snow covers the ground, the arctic hare's cinnamon-colored summer coat turns to white. Only its extremities do not change color with the seasons. Its ear tips are always black, and its tail remains a white "cotton ball." On the permanently frozen arctic tundra, the hares remain white year-round.

In North America, arctic hares live singly and in small groups. Their population varies from year to year. However, the species is getting rarer. In Europe and Asia, arctic hares gather in larger groups. By joining together the hares have a better chance of avoiding sneak attacks from predators such as the arctic fox. When pursued, the hares can run at speeds up to 45 miles per hour. Still, many are caught by foxes and birds of prey.

The female arctic hare gives birth two or three times a year. She keeps her babies hidden for about a month, typically in a burrow or tunnel or among stones or bushes. Many other types of hare breed when they are just six months old, but the arctic hare does not breed until it is a year old.

Hartebeest
Alcelaphus buselaphus

Length: 6 to 8 feet
Weight: 297 to 440 pounds (male); 264 to 396 pounds (female)
Diet: grass

Number of Young: 1
Home: central Africa from Guinea to Ethiopia
Order: Even-toed ungulates
Family: Bovines

 Grasslands

 Mammals

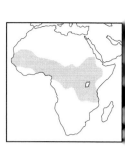

© CARL & ANN PURCELL / CORBIS

The hartebeest is the most common antelope in Africa. Once thought to range the entire continent, it is now found primarily in the open plains of central Africa. Its range has been reduced partly by human encroachment and partly by environmental and climatic changes. A swift and slender antelope, the hartebeest was named for its strength and endurance.

The hartebeest lives in small herds, up to 15 animals, with one male per herd. They establish rigid social ranking within the heard and equally rigid territorial lines. The male marks his territory by standing poised like a statue on some high point, often on a termite mound, where he can see approaching males. If a strange male intrudes, the resident male gallops past him, turns, stops, and threatens with his horns. He repeats this action until the intruder moves out of his territory. Breeding season extends from mid-April to mid-May. The male leaves the herd until the females are ready to mate. A female can mate successfully only one day a year. A single calf is born eight months later. At first the calf does not follow the herd. Instead, it lies motionless on the ground for about two weeks, while the male keeps watch.

The hartebeest is a brown animal whose back slopes downward from heavy front legs. Its face is narrow and elongated. The horns vary in shape, but are present in both sexes. Hartebeests often mingle with other herds of antelope or with zebras.

Hunter's Hartebeest (Hirola)
Beatragus hunteri

Length: 47 to 78 inches
Height at the Shoulder: 40 inches
Weight: 160 pounds
Diet: grasses and herbs

Number of Young: 1
Home: Kenya and Somalia
Order: Even-toed hoofed mammals
Family: Bovines

 Grasslands

 Mammals

© WILLIAM ROBINSON / ANIMALS ANIMALS / EARTH SCENES

In the early-morning coolness of the dry African savanna, small groups of antelope called hirolas gather to graze on the tall grass and drink from a water hole. Hirolas prefer this time of day to the heat of the afternoon, when they rest under tress and in other shady spots. And even though it's quiet on the savanna, the hirolas remain alert, using their keen senses of sight, hearing, and smell to detect any danger. At the first sign on a lion or other predator, the hirolas flee. Like all antelope, they run quickly and gracefully. If a hirola is cornered by a predator, it uses its long, sharp-tipped horns to defend itself. Male hirolas also use their horns to fight one anther during mating season.

Hirolas have reddish-brown fur that grows darker on their legs. Their long, hairy tail is white with a blackish tip. Their faces are distinguished by a well-defined chevron between their eyes. The babies are well developed at birth. Within a few hours, they are able to stand and follow their mother.

Hirolas were once quite numerous in eastern Africa. But as people raised more and more cattle, there was less room for the hirolas. Also, big-game hunters killed many of these creatures for trophies, and their population has consequently decreased. They are now considered among the rarest of Africa's antelope.

Broad-bordered Bee Hawkmoth
Hemaris fuciformis

Diet: flower nectar (adult moth); leaves and stems (caterpillar)
Method of Reproduction: egg layer

Wingspan: 1¼ to 1¾ inches
Home: Europe, Asia, and northern Africa
Order: Butterflies and moths
Family: Hawkmoths

 Cities, Towns, and Farms

 Arthropods

© IAN ROSE / FRANK LANE PICTURE AGENCY / CORBIS

The broad-bordered bee hawkmoth is a member of the unusual sphinx-, or hawk-, moth family. The name "sphinx" refers to the caterpillar, which rears up on its "haunches" in a position similar to the Great Sphinx of Egypt. The name "hawk" refers to the fast, strong flight of the adult moth. Surprisingly, this powerful moth has rather small wings; but it can beat them extremely fast, much like a hummingbird.

In appearance the bee hawkmoth's transparent wings resemble those of a bumblebee. The moths also sound like buzzing bees when they hover in one place. The hawkmoth has a band of dark-colored scales that runs along the edges of its front wings. As the moth flies, it loses some of its wing scales. Older moths may have greatly reduced wing borders. This species is also noted for its strong, thick antennae.

This hawkmoth breaks out of its cocoon, or pupa, in May and flies until June. It is active during the day, usually in bright sunshine. As it zooms about gardens, it stops to hover over flowers, dipping its body to sip the nectar. The female usually lays her eggs on bedstraw, honeysuckle, and snowberry bushes. The eggs hatch into caterpillars that feed on the bush's leaves. A full-grown caterpillar is about 2 inches long and light green or red, with long dark green stripes.

Algerian Hedgehog
Erinaceus algirus

Length: 9 to 11 inches
Weight: 1⅓ to 1¾ pounds
Diet: insects, spiders, worms, small birds, rodents, and fruits
Number of Young: 2 to 10

Home: France, Spain, northern Africa, and the Canary and Balearic Islands
Order: Insectivores
Family: Hedgehogs

 Cities, Towns, and Farms

Mammals

© MARTIN HARVEY / PETER ARNOLD, INC.

The Algerian hedgehog is a slightly smaller version of the familiar European hedgehog, which many of us know from childhood storybooks. But while Beatrix Potter's hedgehogs cook oat porridge, real-life hedgehogs prowl through the night in search of small animals and insects to eat. The Algerian hedgehog also has quite a sweet tooth. Unfortunately, this makes it a serious pest in the Mediterranean, where it steals figs and other orchard fruits. During the day the Algerian hedgehog sleeps curled on its side, huddled under a large tree root, nestled in a bed of leaves or, as you might expect, hidden in a hedge.

To discourage predators, the Algerian hedgehog has as many as 10,000 long, sharp quills. Like all true hedgehogs, this species has a special muscle that extends around its body. When the hedgehog tightens this muscle, the spines on its back pop up, and the hedgehog rolls into a ball. Its soft belly is then safely hidden in the center of the prickly ball. Only a few natural predators, such as owls and some clever foxes, can open a rolled-up hedgehog.

Newborn hedgehogs grow spines even before their eyes are open. The young get along peacefully at first and can often be seen sitting in a neat row, waiting for their mother. But by the time Algerian hedgehogs are a year old, they become quite quarrelsome. As adults, they live solitary lives, except for a brief union at mating time.

Little Blue Heron
Egretta caerulea

Length: about 2 feet
Weight: about 12 ounces
Home: eastern United States
south to central South
America

Diet: mainly fish
Number of Eggs: 2 to 5
Order: Stilt-legged birds
Family: Herons and bitterns

 Fresh Water

 Birds

© TIM ZUROWSKI / CORBIS

The little blue heron is a familiar sight near the marshes, ponds, and lakes of the eastern United States. Although the East is its home, the little blue heron is a wanderer. It occasionally appears in the western states and has been known to nest in California.

The little blue heron is a skilled angler that can catch surprisingly large fish for its small size. It stalks its prey by standing motionless in shallow water, waiting patiently to strike. The young herons do not fish nearly as skillfully as the older birds. During their first year, young herons often miss their targets or blunder clumsily through the water, scaring away their prey. When fish are difficult to catch or just scarce, little blues eat insects, worms, and other invertebrates.

Immature little blue herons are not blue at all, but white, with gray wing tips. When the young birds darken to a grayish-blue, they are old enough to mate. In spring the mature males initiate courtship by flying in large circles above their chosen mates. Landing near a female, a male will stretch his long neck and clapper his bill noisily. If the attraction is mutual, the two birds rub bills and preen each other's feathers. Together, they build a small, flimsy nest in a shrub or low tree over some water. This fragile platform of sticks and twigs contains a little hollow at the center for several bluish-green eggs.

Nankeen Night Heron
Nycticorax caledonicus

Length: about 2 feet
Weight: 1½ to 2 pounds
Diet: fish, frogs, crustaceans, and insects
Number of Eggs: 2 to 5

Home: Australia, Indonesia, and other South Pacific islands
Order: Stilt-legged birds
Family: Herons and bitterns

Fresh Water

Birds

© JOHN SHAW / BRUCE COLEMAN INC.

Each evening the nankeen night heron begins its search for food just as other herons are returning to their roosts to sleep. Because it is nocturnal, this heron is seldom seen. Yet it is one of the most common herons in Australia. During the day, nankeens sleep together in leafy trees, often in city parks. Their nighttime feeding grounds may be some distance away.

Although they sleep side by side during the day, nankeen night herons are less social at night. Generally each forages in a separate feeding area near a river or lake. Nankeens hunt for frogs and small fish in shallow water near shore. Occasionally, however, they actually jump or dive into the water to catch their prey. Nankeens also scavenge beneath trees where other waterbirds nest, gobbling down fallen eggs and chicks.

These herons breed year round, usually in colonies. Both males and females share in nest building: the male fetches the sticks, and the female assembles them into a flimsy platform. The parents also share in the duties of tending the eggs and raising the chicks. Their light green eggs hatch about three weeks after they are laid.

The nankeen night heron is named for the cinnamon color of its feathers. The bird's plumage reminded early European settlers of a popular type of brown cotton cloth that came from Nanking, China.

13

Purple Heron
Ardea purpurea

Length: 30 to 36 inches
Wingspan: 48 to 60 inches
Weight: 20 to 40 ounces
Diet: mainly fish and insects
Number of Eggs: 3 to 5

Home: Europe, Asia, and Africa
Order: Stilt-legged birds
Family: Herons and bitterns

Fresh Water

Birds

© PETER JOHNSON / CORBIS

The colorful purple heron is one of Europe's most unsocial long-legged wading birds. Extremely shy and frightened of humans, it nests and feeds hidden among thick stands of bulrushes and other tall reeds. Its dark gray wings and striped body are well camouflaged in the high vegetation. When alarmed by an intruder, the heron stretches its snakelike neck and points its long bill to the sky. In this position the slender bird is nearly impossible to see among the tall reeds. There it remains, standing motionless, until the danger passes.

Although the purple heron often finds all the food it needs in one hidden place, it is able to fly long distances. A rare glimpse of this bird high in the air is usually the only sign that it lives in the area. From a distance a purple heron in flight can be mistaken for the more familiar gray heron. However, purple herons are identified by their long, "S"-shaped neck, which droops down in an obvious bulge while the birds are flying.

The heron is most active in the early morning and early evening hours. A solitary hunter, it may patiently stand on a mat of floating plants or slowly wade through the water. When it spots its prey, the heron strikes out with lightning speed, capturing a fish or insect and swallowing it in one gulp. The purple heron also eats an occasional frog, snake, or other small animal.

Pygmy Hog
Sus salvanius

Length of the Body: 1¾ to 2⅓ feet

Length of the Tail: 8 to 14½ inches

Height at the Shoulder: 8 to 12 inches

Weight: 14½ to 26 pounds

Diet: plants and small animals

Number of Young: 2 to 6

Home: India

Order: Even-toed hoofed mammals

Family: Old World pigs

 Grasslands

 Mammals

Endangered Animals

© TOM MCHUGH / PHOTO RESEARCHERS

People who have traveled to India often remark upon the elephant grass, a type of grass that grows as tall as an adult human. Few humans would try to make their way through these dense, nearly junglelike stands. But what seems impossible for a human to penetrate is home sweet home to the pygmy hog, a harmless little creature that now stands in grave danger of extinction. The pygmy hog's forbidding habitat has been all but destroyed, making the animal easy prey for hunters who savor its tender meat.

Those few pygmy hogs that remain spend their days slipping between the tough grass stems in an unending search for food. Like all pigs, the pygmy hog is not a picky eater, dining on whatever's available. Its preferred food seems to be leaves, fruits, roots, and other plant matter, although the pygmy hog never turns its snout up at earthworms, bird eggs, insects, or even the rotting flesh of dead animals.

Each pygmy hog builds itself a cavelike nest in which to sleep and as a haven against predators and bad weather. The creature goes about its nest building in a very businesslike manner. First it uses its snout and front hooves to scoop out a depression in the ground. Then the hog fills the depression with a large pile of grass. Finally the creature hollows out a nest in the center of the pile.

Red-billed Hornbill
Tockus erythrorhynchus

Length: about 18 inches
Weight: about 5 ounces
Diet: insects and fruits
Number of Eggs: 3 to 5

Home: Africa
Order: Kingfishers and their relatives
Family: Hornbills

 Forests and Mountains

 Birds

© MARTIN B. WITHERS / FRANK LANE PICTURE AGENCY / CORBIS

Red-billed hornbills have an extraordinary way of nesting and raising their chicks. The female lays a clutch of eggs in a tree hole. Then she seals herself inside, with help from the male on the outside. The pair barricades the nest with bits of mud, leaving a small slit through which the male can pass food. Although the female is unable to gather food, she is almost totally protected from predators. She keeps her tiny house in good order by throwing leftovers out of the tiny nest hole. She also uses the hole as a sort of "tree toilet," making her droppings fall to the ground.

While the female incubates the eggs, she molts, or loses her feathers. By the time the chicks are several days old, the mother's feathers have regrown. She then uses her strong, sharp bill to hack her way out of the nest. Her young—not yet ready to fly—seal themselves up again. By this time, both parents must work around the clock to feed their rapidly growing chicks. Once they are ready to fly, the chicks break free with help from their parents.

Red-billed hornbills live in mated pairs and small families in Africa's bushlands and sparsely planted woods. There they hunt for fruit and insects. Redbills are noted for their large beak, which is flattened from side to side. But their beak lacks the large, horny bump, or "casque," seen on other hornbills. Both sexes look similar, although the male is somewhat larger.

16

Large Horntail
Urocerus gigas

Length: up to 1½ inches
Wingspan: about 3 inches
Diet: tree wood
Method of Reproduction: egg layer

Home: Eurasia, northern Africa, North America, and Brazil
Order: Wasps, ants, and bees
Family: Horntails

 Cities, Towns, and Farms

 Arthropods

© PETER BAUMANN / ANIMALS ANIMALS / EARTH SCENES

The large horntail is also called the giant wood wasp, for an obvious reason. To lay her eggs, the female inserts her "ovipositor," a long, flexible organ on the back of her body, into a piece of wood. Through it, she deposits the eggs, sometimes as deep as one inch. On rare occasions the female horntail cannot pull out again and dies stuck in a branch or piece of lumber.

In nature, large horntails lay their eggs only in sick or damaged trees. Unfortunately, they also deposit their eggs in lumber and buildings. The young, wormlike wasps, or larvae, develop inside the wood. When they are ready to emerge as adult wasps, they bore to the surface.

This boring can do great damage. For instance, large horntails emerging from telephone poles have been known to chew straight through metal cables. Large horntails in buildings will cut through plaster walls and carpeting in their frenzy to escape. Sometimes their boring weakens a wall to the point of collapse.

Luckily, horntail worms have some natural enemies. Some species of parasite wasps have ovipositors just as long as the adult horntail's. These wasps bore through the wood to deposit their eggs on the bodies of developing horntail larvae. When the eggs hatch, the parasite wasps eat and kill the young horntails.

Przewalski's Horse
Equus przewalskii

Length: 7 to 9 feet
Height: 3¼ to 5 feet
Weight: 450 to 750 pounds
Diet: grasses
Number of Young: 1

Home: western Mongolia
Order: Odd-toed hoofed mammals
Family: Horses

 Grasslands

 Mammals

© BRYAN KNOX / PAPILIO / CORBIS

? Endangered Animals

Przewalski's horse is the last real wild horse. Until the 1900s, it lived in the dry plateaus of Mongolia and China. Nikolay Przewalski, a Russian traveler, discovered the small horse in 1879. Today Przewalski's horses only exist in zoos, and they number about 400.

Przewalski's horse is thought to be an ancestor of the domestic horse. You can tell it apart from other horses because it is smaller and has a larger head and a shorter mane that stands straight up. The horse was domesticated 6,000 years ago. Prehistoric humans, known today as the Cro-Magnons, painted and carved images of these wild horses on walls in caves in France and Spain 17,000 years ago.

In the wild, the horse ate the sparse and tough grasses of the steppes. Each small herd was ruled by a head stallion that protected it, attacked intruders, and fought off rival males. The young, called foals, are born in the spring. If the weather turns cold, adult horses form a circle around the foals to keep them warm.

In the fall, the horses shed their old coats and grow thicker ones, which they need to protect them from the cold and the winter wind. When water holes froze, the wild horses quenched their thirst by eating snow. They lived on grass they uncovered by digging in the snow.

Cattle Horsefly
Tabanus bovinus

Length: 1 inch or less
Diet: female: blood of mammals; male: nectar and pollen; larva: insects
Method of Reproduction: egg layer

Home: Europe, Asia, and North Africa
Order: Flies and mosquitoes
Family: Horseflies and deerflies

 Cities, Towns, and Farms

 Arthropods

© HERBERT SCHWIND / OKAPIA / PHOTO RESEARCHERS

When a female cattle horsefly's large, bulging eyes spot a horse grazing in a field, it knows a tasty meal is in the offing. The horsefly swoops down toward the horse, its wings making a loud "whir-r-r" sound as it circles its victim. If the horse moves away, the fly chases it. When the fly finally settles, it pierces the horse's skin with its tough mouthparts and begins to feed on the horse's blood. As the fly feeds, some of its saliva is injected into the blood. The saliva contains chemicals that prevent the horse's blood from clotting while the fly is feeding.

The cattle horsefly's bite is painful, but there is little that the horse can do. The fly bites in an area out of reach of the horse's head and tail. Open sores often develop where female horseflies feed—usually on the neck, back, and legs of the horse. The sores do not heal because the flies return over and over again to feed in the same spots.

Female cattle horseflies also attack cattle and other domestic animals. Unlike other species of horseflies, they seldom attack people. In contrast to the female, the male cattle horsefly is harmless. It feeds mainly on nectar, a sugary liquid produced by plants. In the process, it can be helpful by carrying its pollen from one flower to another, thereby aiding the process of pollination.

Cape Hyrax
Procavia capensis

Length: up to 2 feet
Weight: up to 3 pounds
Diet: fruits, leaves, and other
vegetation

Number of Young: 2 to 3
Home: southern Africa
Order: Hyraxes
Family: Hyraxes

 Grasslands

 Mammals

© D. ROBERT & LORRI FRANZ / CORBIS

Cape hyraxes are a strange little animals. With their short brown fur and plump bodies, they look much like guinea pigs. These 3-pound mammals have some interesting body features—there are suction cups on the soles of their feet and tiny hoofs on their toes!

Cape hyraxes live in southern Africa. They make their homes atop rocky cliffs or among boulders in the plains. They are very sociable and live in colonies of 50 or more animals. On warm, sunny days, large groups of hyraxes climb onto rocky ledges to bask in the sun. but they always post guards to keep a watch out for leopards, wild dogs, eagles, hawks, and other enemies. If one approaches, a guard lets out a loud, shrill cry. But if all is calm, the hyraxes continue to chirp cheerfully among themselves. In addition to sunning themselves in a group, hyraxes also eat together. Their food consists mostly of leaves, grasses, shrubs, and other plant life abundant on the African savanna.

Most small female animals have very short pregnancies. But hyraxes are pregnant for seven and half months. When the babies are born, they begin jumping around within a few hours. The females carry the babies around on their backs for two months, until the young are old enough to forage for food themselves.

Rufous-tailed Jacamar
Galbula ruficauda

Length: 9 to 11 inches
Weight: about 1 ounce
Number of Eggs: 2 or 3
Home: Mexico, Central America, and South America

Diet: insects
Order: Woodpeckers, toucans, and honeyguides
Family: Jacamars

 Rainforests

 Birds

© FRANCOIS GOHIER / PHOTO RESEARCHERS

This colorful tropical bird is named for its long, reddish tail. Even more brilliant is its gleaming jacket of green feathers. Male and female jacamars are equally beautiful. The male sports a cream-colored throat, while the female's is coppery.

The rufous-tailed jacamar is a graceful, acrobatic flier. It zooms and darts after insects, particularly butterflies, snapping them up in midair. Usually the bird waits to eat until it has returned to its perch. If the insect is still struggling, the jacamar may smash it against a tree branch to kill it. Jacamars are also careful to scrape off any hard shells or spiny legs before swallowing their insect meal.

Like its relative the woodpecker, the jacamar's toes face in opposite directions. Two toes on each foot point forward, and two point backward. This gives the jacamar an extrafirm grip that allows it to walk up and down a tree trunk headfirst.

Rufous-tailed jacamars are remarkable for their habit of digging underground nests. The female does most of the work, hollowing out a nesting tunnel and depositing eggs at the end of it. However, her mate then helps tend to the eggs and chicks. Generally the female sits on the eggs at night, and the male takes over during the day. Nineteen to 23 days after the eggs are laid, they hatch.

Wattled Jacana
Jacana jacana

Length: 9 to 12 inches
Weight: 3½ to 5 ounces
Number of Eggs: usually 4
Home: Central and South America

Diet: mainly insects
Order: Waders and gull-like birds
Family: Jacanas

Fresh Water

Birds

© LUIZ C. MARINO / PETER ARNOLD, INC.

The wattled jacana's extremely long toes and claws work like snowshoes, distributing the bird's weight over a very large surface. Such extraordinary feet enable the bird to walk across lily pads and thin mats of floating vegetation without sinking.

These birds can be found in Central and South American swamps and marshes, and along the edges of thickly planted streams. While searching for food, they often use their beak to flip over floating lily pads, picking worms and insects off the exposed roots. Occasionally jacanas catch small frogs and fish just beneath the water surface.

Females are very territorial and often fight among themselves for a spot of land.

The larger bird usually drives away the smaller one and then breeds with the loser's mate. Female jacanas often have up to four mates during a breeding season. Nest building is largely left to the male. His flimsy structure is often no more than a mound of water plants tossed in place and stamped down. The female lays her eggs in one or more nests and usually helps to incubate them.

Many experts believe that the wattled jacana is the same species as the North American jacana, a familiar bird in Texas, the Caribbean islands, and Central America. As adults, both types of jacanas are handsomely marked in red and brown. But the wattled jacana is somewhat larger.

22

Black-backed Jackal
Canis mesomelas

Length: 37 to 54 inches (including the tail)
Height at the Shoulder: 18 to 20 inches
Weight: 20 to 30 pounds

Diet: plants and animals
Number of Young: up to 9
Home: Africa
Order: Carnivores
Family: Dogs

  Grasslands

Mammals

© PAUL A. SOUDERS / CORBIS

Black-backed jackals are noisy creatures. They communicate with one another by means of screams, yaps, howls, and other sounds. "Ke-ke-ke-kek!" is an alarm call used to warn that lions are prowling nearby. "Wuf" is a soft call made by parents when an enemy approaches their pups. "Bweha!" is a howl followed by short yelps; it is heard in the evening or at night, while the jackals hunt.

Black-backed jackals usually hunt alone or with one companion. But 20 or more jackals may gather around and devour the remains of an animal killed by a lion, cheetah, or other large carnivore. Jackals locate these kills by watching vultures circle high in the sky. When the vultures swoop to the ground, the jackals know the birds spotted something to eat. They rush to the place the vultures found. Often a lion is busy eating. The jackals and vultures—often joined by hyenas—wait nearby. Slowly, they move closer and closer to the lion. Sometimes they annoy the lion so much that it leaves, even though it hasn't finished eating. Black-backed jackals also eat rodents, birds, snakes, insects, eggs, fruits, and berries. In some places, jackals are pests because they attack and eat farm animals.

The female black-backed jackal gives birth in a den or burrow. For the first three weeks of their life, pups feed only on their mother's milk. Then the parents begin to bring the pups meat. When the pups are about eight weeks old, they start to join their parents on hunting trips and slowly learn the art of the kill.

Trumpet-stalked Jellyfish (Stauromedusan)
Haliclystus salpinx

Length: about 1 inch
Diet: small shrimp and large zooplankton
Method of Reproduction: egg layer

Home: coastal Atlantic waters from New Brunswick to Cape Cod
Order: Stalked jellyfishes
Family: Stalked jellyfishes

 Oceans and Shores

Other Invertebrates

© WILLIAM H. AMOS / PHOTO RESEARCHERS

Most jellyfish swim quite fast with their arms trailing behind them. But stauromedusans move slowly and attach themselves to marine plants, rocks, and other underwater objects. These unusual little jellyfish are found only in cold ocean waters.

A familiar North American stauromedusan is the trumpet-stalked jellyfish. It anchors its trumpet-shaped body onto seaweed or a rock using its sticky center stalk. The stalk ends in a suction cup. This stauromedusan is also called the clown jellyfish, after its bright colors. The species can be found in bright red, orange, yellow, or tan. Whatever its color, the body is partly transparent, or "translucent," letting light pass through it.

The trumpet-stalked jellyfish has eight short arms that surround the center stalk. Each arm ends with a starburst of bright tentacles. Buds at the end of each tentacle contain a mild, stinging chemical that the jellyfish uses to stun its prey. Once it has snagged a meal, the jellyfish simply bends its arms toward its mouth. The mouth, located at the center of the jellyfish's body, has four distinct lips.

The trumpet-stalked jellyfish moves slowly, inching along a blade of eelgrass or other solid object. The creature gets from place to place by alternately moving its center stalk and the many small "anchor tentacles" between its arms.

European John Dory
Zeus faber

Length: up to 2 feet
Diet: small fish
Method of Reproduction: egg layer

Home: eastern Atlantic Ocean and Mediterranean Sea
Order: Dories and boarfishes
Family: Dories

Oceans and Shores

Fish

© ROY WALLER / NHPA

The European John Dory has been considered a delicacy since Roman times. Today it is caught in huge nets from commercial fishing boats and sold at markets around the world.

The French word for dory, *dorée*, means "gilded in gold." Some of these fish are golden in color, and all have yellow-rimmed black blotches, one on each side. The European John Dory is also called the St. Peter's fish. According to legend, the black spots on the fish's sides are St. Peter's fingerprints.

A John Dory feeds by slurping up smaller fish. It engulfs them whole—sometimes several at a time—because it can stretch out its mouth to a remarkable size. The John Dory hunts in small groups, usually in deep water not too far from the coast.

A closely related and possibly identical species, *Zeus capensis*, is found throughout the South Seas. This southern John Dory is caught in great quantities off the coasts of southern Africa, Australia, and New Zealand. Some scientists say that the two species are really one and the same. Both fish are flabby, with bodies that are flattened from side to side. They all have 10 long, delicate spines on the dorsal fin (the fin on top of the back). These spines often become ripped and torn, giving the adult John Dory a rather ratty-looking appearance.

Steppe Katydid
Ephippigen vitium

Length: 1 to 1¼ inches
Length of the Wing: ³⁄₁₆ inch
Diet: leaves and small insects
Method of Reproduction: egg layer

Home: western Europe
Order: Grasshoppers and their relatives
Family: Katydids

  Forests and Mountains

Arthropods

The steppe katydid has wings, but it cannot fly. Instead, it uses its stubby wings to sing. Its wings are curved and have ridges like the teeth of a comb. The two wings fit one inside the other like two bowls. When the steppe katydid moves its wings back and forth, the ridges rub and make a sound.

Like katydids in North America, the European steppe katydid sings to attract a mate. During the summer, its high-pitched call can get quite loud. Among North American katydids, only the males make noise. But both male and female steppe katydids can sing. There is one slight difference between the sexes: Male steppe katydids use their left wings to scrape the ridges on their right wings. But the females use their right wings to scrape the ridges on their left ones. Perhaps the male and female steppe katydids can hear the difference. The male steppe katydid also makes a drumming sound. He does this by rapidly beating his hard belly against a branch.

After mating, the female steppe katydid deposits her eggs in a hole in the ground. The eggs, about ⅛ of an inch long when they are laid, remain buried through the winter. The following year a new batch of katydids emerges, crawls up into the trees, and begins the annual symphony. Although they cannot fly, steppe katydids are powerful jumpers.

Prairie Kingsnake
Lampropeltis calligaster

Length: 2½ to 4½ feet
Diet: birds, frogs, small rodents, lizards, and other snakes
Method of Reproduction: egg layer

Home: Maryland to Florida and west to Nebraska and Texas
Order: Lizards and snakes
Family: Colubrid snakes

Cities, Towns, and Farms

Reptiles

© JOSEPH T. COLLINS / PHOTO RESEARCHERS

The prairie kingsnake often crosses rural roads on warm spring and summer evenings. Occasionally it ventures out during the day, flushed from its hiding place by a strong rainstorm. Otherwise the snake sleeps the day away, wedged under a rock or buried beneath a layer of loose dirt. Sometimes it beds down in a rodent burrow—after eating the inhabitant. This slender but muscular snake is a powerful constrictor. It suffocates its prey before swallowing the victim whole.

Within their large range, prairie kingsnakes are found in a variety of colors and patterns. In general, they are a muted shade of brown. The handsomest individuals have large dark brown, reddish-brown, or greenish spots down the center of the back. These oval-shaped blotches are often bordered in black. Two rows of smaller spots may run down the snake's sides. The snakes tend to grow darker as they age, old ones becoming a uniform dark brown.

The snake's original habitat—the open prairie—has largely disappeared. But the species continues to thrive in open fields, pastures, and farm country, and in rocky hillsides and dry woodlands.

In June or July, the female digs a hole in the ground in which she lays her eggs. When they hatch 7 to 11 days later, the newborn are up to a foot long.

27

Greater Kudu
Tragelaphus strepsiceros

Length of the Body: 6 to 8 feet
Length of the Tail: 12 to 22 inches
Weight: 400 to 780 pounds
Diet: leaves, grasses, and herbs

Number of Young: 1
Home: eastern and southern Africa
Order: Even-toed hoofed mammals
Family: Bovines

 Grasslands

 Mammals

© MICHAEL CALLAN / FRANK LANE PICTURE AGENCY / CORBIS

The greater kudu is called the "king of the antelope" in honor of the stately horns worn by old males, called bulls. The 5-foot-long, widely spread horns of a full-grown male form two or three complete spiral twists. It may take many years for a young bull to reach such majesty. The males often duel with their horns, both seriously and playfully. Older bulls sometimes wrestle by interlocking their horns and pushing against each other. Occasionally their horns lock together so tightly that neither bull can escape, and both die.

Many years ago, enormous herds of greater kudu roamed the African savannas. But game hunters killed a great many bulls for their magnificent horns. A disease made matters worse, wiping out thousands of kudus at the end of the 19th century. As a result, the greater kudu has disappeared from much of Africa. Most now live only in southwestern Africa, where herds often gather around farm wells. Greater kudus can jump 8-foot fences, so farmers build towering fences to keep kudus off their land.

Typically a kudu herd consists of five to 20 animals—mainly females, their calves, and young bulls. Older bulls tend to be solitary or live in bachelor herds. They join the female herds only during mating season. The herds graze quietly on the leaves and shoots of a large variety of plants, including bitter-tasting herbs rejected by other antelope.

Lesser Kudu
Tragelaphus imberbis

Length of the Body: 4 feet
Length of the Tail: 10 to 16 inches
Height at the Shoulder: 3 feet
Diet : leaves, herbs, grasses, and fruits

Weight: up to 230 pounds
Number of Young: 1
Home: eastern Africa
Order: Even-toed hoofed mammals
Family: Bovines

 Grasslands

 Mammals

© RENEE LYNN / PHOTO RESEARCHERS

The magnificent 3-foot-long horns of the lesser kudu are half as large as those of the greater kudu, its massive cousin. In many other respects as well, the lesser kudu is a smaller version of its close relative. Since its smaller size makes it no match for predators, the lesser kudu must use its great speed and agility to escape danger. Always ready to flee from predators, the kudu warn each other of danger by barking loudly.

Adult males and females look quite different from one another. The buck (male) is easily distinguished by his spiral horns and by the short mane that runs down the nape of his neck. The sexes also differ in color. The bucks are dark bluish gray, while the does (females) are a light reddish brown with white stripes. Lesser kudu are neither social nor territorial. Most does form lifelong friendships with only two or three other does. Within these small female groups, they raise their young. Most grown bulls live solitary lives. They are allowed to join female groups only to mate.

Lesser kudu are much less common today than they were at the beginning of the century. This is because their habitat has been greatly disturbed by humans and domestic livestock. Also, hunters kill countless kudu for their beautiful horns. Fortunately, many lesser kudu now live in protected national parks.

Common Langur
Presbytis entellus

Length of the Body: 1½ to 3½ feet
Length of the Tail: 2½ to 3½ feet
Weight: 20 to 46 pounds (male); 16 to 40 pounds (female)

Diet: plants and insects
Number of Young: 1 or 2
Home: India
Order: Primates
Family: Old World monkeys
Subfamily: Langurs and colobi

Rainforests

Mammals

?

Endangered Animals

© KEVIN SCHAFER / CORBIS

In India, many people worship the common langur as an incarnation, or living form, of the Hindu god Hanuman. To understand why, you only have to see one of these humanlike monkeys sitting at rest. Its posture is erect and dignified, much like that of a wise old man, or even an ape-god.

Because they are so well loved by native people, common langurs often climb about undisturbed on the roofs and walls of homes and temples. They know, from centuries of experience, that they will not be harmed and will often be fed. Nonetheless, this species is endangered because so much of its rainforest home has been destroyed.

In the wild, common langurs seem to be equally at home in trees and on the ground, but they prefer to live near water. Like all langurs, this species is acrobatic and will leap from branch to branch in the treetops.

Common langurs are found in a variety of social groups that vary in size from eight to more than 100 animals. Most commonly, one male lives with several females and their young. The family members share in toting the newborns about, and it may be more than an hour before a child is returned to its mother. Some extended families include two or three adult males of different ages and ranks. Common langurs also form "boy clubs," made up of males of all ages.

Lapwing
Vanellus vanellus

Length: 12 inches
Number of Eggs: 3 to 5
Home: Europe, Asia, and northwestern Africa

Diet: mainly insects
Order: Water birds
Family: Plovers

Cities, Towns, and Farms

Birds

© NIALL BENVIE / CORBIS

The lapwing, with its sparkling-green "jacket" and tall, fancy "hat," is the prettiest bird in its family, a group called plovers. These wading birds all have a stubby bill, a rounded head, and short legs. The lapwing is quite unusual among wading birds, because it often lives far from rivers, lakes, and oceans. This plump but lively bird loves open spaces and prefers to live on grasslands and farm fields.

Also known as the peewit, the lapwing makes a loud, nasal cry, "pee-r-weet," when it flies. In spring, the breeding season, lapwings perform wild, acrobatic display flights. They zigzag through the air erratically, plunging headlong toward the ground and then slowly flapping upward

again. The male lapwing tries to win the favor of a female with his acrobatics. If he succeeds, he scrapes a shallow nest hole in the ground. His mate then lines the nest with grass and moss. She lays her eggs and warms them until they hatch, about four weeks later. The chicks are not as colorful as their parents. Sometime between their first and second year, the young grow long head crests and colorful body feathers.

In winter, lapwings gather in large, noisy flocks that may cover several fields. When cold weather makes insects scarce, the birds supplement their diet with plants. As soon as the ground thaws in spring, they begin to search for worms, snails, and newly hatched insect larvae.

Gentle Gray Lemur
Hapalemur griseus

Length of the Body: about 16 inches
Length of the Tail: about 16 inches
Diet: mainly bamboo shoots and leaves

Weight: about 2 pounds
Number of Young: 1
Home: Madagascar
Order: Primates
Family: Lemurs

 Rainforests

 Mammals

© TOM & PAT LEESON / PHOTO RESEARCHERS

? Endangered Animals

The gentle gray lemur's babylike face and quiet personality make it an especially sought-after pet. Sadly, *wild* lemurs are not so valued. Their habitat has been destroyed, and they have been hunted to near extinction.

These primates live in small family groups among bamboo thickets and reeds. There they forage for food in early morning and at dusk. Adult lemurs perfume their fur and their surroundings with an oil from their body that smells like beeswax.

Lemur parents are very affectionate with their single baby. First the mother carries her newborn in her mouth or lets it cling to her belly. Later the baby rides on her back or on its father's back. When the youngster is about two weeks old, it follows its parents from place to place. By then it knows to hide from danger by lying flat on the ground, "disappearing " among the reeds.

One of the largest populations of gently gray lemurs lives near Lake Alaotra in Madagascar, an island off southeastern Africa. Unfortunately, farmers are converting the lake area to rice paddies. Also, local people hunt the lemurs by burning the reeds where the animals live. The good news is that gentle lemurs are expanding their numbers in other places. Luckily, they live in harmony with the native people who inhabit jungle areas.

California Legless Lizard
Anniella pulchra

Length: 6 to 9 inches
Number of Young: 1 to 4
Home: western California and Baja California

Diet: insects and their larvae
Order: Lizards and snakes
Family: California legless lizards

 Grasslands

 Reptiles

© TOM MCHUGH / PHOTO RESEARCHERS

Most people could easily mistake this long, slender lizard for a snake. But experts identify it as a legless lizard by its angular head and blunt tail. Although legless, the lizard has remnants of its legged ancestor—shoulder bones and hipbones within its streamlined body. Scientists place California legless lizards in a family by themselves. They are most closely related to the glass and alligator lizards of the anguid family. But the California species lacks the anguids' external ears and bony armor.

Over millions of years, this shiny lizard evolved a legless body, perfectly suited to life underground. Its smooth scales and blunt tail enable it to move backward and forward in the dirt. California legless lizards live in grassy sand dunes, along the gravelly banks of small streams, and beneath the loose soil of farm fields and open forests. They seldom emerge above ground.

Active at night, the lizards hunt for buried insects and their grubs. They mate in May and June, and their young are born live in fall. Most of these lizards are silvery on top, with a yellow belly and dark stripes along the back and sides. A subspecies of black-and-brown legless lizard lives along the California coast. Unfortunately, pesticides have poisoned entire populations, so the lizard has disappeared from many parts of its former range.

Common Cape Girdled Lizard
Cordylus cordylus

Length: about 7½ inches
Diet: mainly insects; occasionally slugs and smaller lizards

Number of Young: 2 to 5
Home: South Africa
Order: Lizards and snakes
Family: Girdle-tailed lizards

Deserts

Reptiles

© HANS REINHARD / BRUCE COLEMAN INC.

The armor of the common Cape girdled lizard protects it from both the drying sun and the creature's toothy enemies. When attacked, the lizard runs headfirst into a rock crevice. All that its enemy can see is the lizard's large, spiny tail, waving dangerously from side to side. The hard spikes on the tail can inflict a painful wound.

Occasionally a brave or foolish predator, such as a dog, will grab the lizard's tail and pull the creature from its hole. This lizard cannot shed its tail and run away, as many reptiles can. Instead, it pulls its armored legs and head close to its flat body and plays dead. Although the lizard appears limp and lifeless, it will strongly resist being flipped over. It instinctively knows that it must protect its soft belly, the most vulnerable part of its body.

Cape girdled lizards are very common throughout southern Africa. They vary in color from orange through brown to black, depending on the region in which they are found. Most have spots for camouflage among the desert rocks.

The Cape girdled lizard is a cold-blooded reptile that tries to avoid the cold of night and the heat of midday. It does so by huddling beneath and between rocks and boulders. In the early morning, the lizard emerges to sun itself. Once its body is warm, it begins to hunt for insects such as beetles, grasshoppers, and termites.

Italian Wall Lizard
Podarcis sicula

Length: 5½ to 9½ inches
Weight: 7 to 10 ounces
Diet: insects, snails, and worms

Number of Eggs: 3 to 8
Home: Europe
Order: Lizards and snakes
Family: Old World lizards

 Cities, Towns, and Farms

Reptiles

© SUZANNE L. & JOSEPH T. COLLINS / PHOTO RESEARCHERS

The Italian wall lizard occurs in large numbers in Italy's famous stone aqueducts, ancient temples, and Roman coliseums. It can also be seen sunning itself on farm buildings and along the sides of roads and highways. Like wall lizards throughout the Old World (Europe, Africa, and Asia), the Italian species functions best at a very high body temperature. So this wall lizard spends lots of time basking in the strong sun to absorb heat.

The Italian wall lizard is a strong climber with powerful hind legs. During the hottest part of the day, it scrambles after insects, snails, and worms. But on cloudy, cold days, this lizard seems to disappear. Without the heat of the sun, it must rest almost motionless inside rock crevices, waiting for a sunnier and warmer day.

This lizard has suffered greatly from the increased use of pesticides. These farm chemicals kill the bugs and slugs that the lizard needs for food. In addition, wall lizards occasionally eat pesticide-poisoned insects. The poisons then build up in the lizard's body, killing it or harming its eggs and offspring.

Female wall lizards lay their eggs under stones or in shallow nests dug in the sand. They cover the eggs carefully, but leave them largely unguarded. After hatching, the young lizards are all drably colored, like their mother. As they mature, the males become much more colorful.

Lyre-headed Lizard
Lyriocephalus scutatus

Length: up to 14 inches
Diet: insects, buds, and tender plant shoots
Number of Eggs: 3 to 9

Home: Sri Lanka
Order: Agamids and chameleons
Family: Agamids

 Rainforests

 Reptiles

© GEORGE GRALL / NGS IMAGE COLLECTION

The adult lyre-headed lizard is recognized by a characteristic thick bump on its snout. This strange bump is filled with spongy tissue and is covered with large, smooth scales. It grows larger as the lizard matures. Scientists are unsure of the bump's purpose. The lizard also has a bony arch, or "brow," over its eyes. These bumpy features give the lizard a profile that resembles the curvy outline of a lyre (an ancient Greek musical instrument)—thus the name.

Male and female lizards look quite different. The male sports a large fold of skin on the back of his neck; another flap of loose skin, called a dewlap, hangs beneath his neck. The female lacks these extra skin folds.

Lyre-headed lizards are found only in the mountainous rainforests of Sri Lanka, an island off the coast of India. People often see them running across the ground in search of insects. The lizards are agile climbers that scramble quickly through the treetops, stopping only occasionally to nibble on tender plants.

The year-round warmth of Sri Lanka allows the lizard to mate at any time. In the course of a year, a single adult male may mate with many females or with one female several times. The female hides her eggs in a shallow scrape that she usually conceals well among grasses and weeds.

Sand Lizard
Lacerta agilis

Length: 8 to 12 inches,
including a 4½- to 7-inch tail
Number of Eggs: 4 to 12
Home: Europe and western
Asia

Diet: insects and spiders
Order: Lizards and snakes
Family: Common Old World
lizards

 Grasslands

 Reptiles

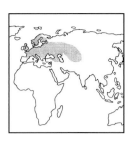

© GEORGE MCCARTHY / CORBIS

Unlike most creatures, the sand lizard depends on its tail to elude its enemies. Should a predator grab a sand lizard by its tail, the tail simply breaks off. Then, although detached from the lizard's body, the amputated tail twitches and coils, distracting the predator long enough for the now-tailless lizard to rush off on its powerful legs. Even though a sand lizard's tail can be longer than its body, losing it does not seem to hurt the creature very much. In fact, within a few months, it grows a new one!

The sand lizard lives in coastal sand dunes and meadows, at the edges of fields and forests, and in parks and gardens. During the winter, it hibernates in holes in the ground. When it emerges in spring, the sand lizard enjoys basking in the warm sunshine. A few weeks later, the breeding season begins. At this time the male sheds his dull winter skin and turns a brilliant green, and a row of white spots appears along each side. After mating, the female digs a hole deep in the sand or soil, lays her eggs in the hole, and then covers them with soil. The heat of the sun incubates the eggs.

The young lizards hatch in 8 to 10 weeks. Although tiny, they look exactly like their parents. At first, they can catch only very small insects and insect larvae. As they get older, they hunt for larger insects. Both adult and young sand lizards feed in morning and late afternoon, avoiding the hot midday sun.

Short-horned Lizard
Phrynosoma douglassi

Length: 2½ to 6 inches
Diet: mainly ants
Method of Reproduction:
    live-bearer

Home: western North America
Order: Lizards and snakes
Family: Iguanas

 Forests and Mountains

Reptiles

© JOE MCDONALD / BRUCE COLEMAN INC.

Horned lizards, commonly nicknamed "horny toads," make up a large group of small iguanas with extremely wide, flat bodies and short, sturdy legs and tails. Horned lizards are especially common in the dry western United States and Mexico. Like its cousins, the short-horned lizard wears a crown of spines across the back of its head. However, its horny crown is stubbier than most and is divided by a deep notch at the back of the skull. The entire crown and head are usually red. The outside edge of the lizard's round body is fringed with a row of pointed scales.

Short-horned lizards thrive in a variety of habitats: from grassy deserts and rocky plains to forests and mountains. The greatest threat to their population is urban development.

Hikers and campers often see "shorthorns" because the iguanas are very active during the day, even in the greatest heat. Like other horned lizards, this species often lives near ant nests, which provide an endless supply of the lizard's favorite food.

A horned lizard's best defense against predators is camouflage. When frightened, it flattens its body against the ground or quickly buries itself under a thin layer of sand. At night, horned lizards burrow into sand and soft dirt for warmth. The shorthorn is unique among horned lizards because it gives birth to live young.

Slender Glass Lizard
Ophisaurus attenuatus

Diet: snails, insects, spiders, and small reptiles
Method of Reproduction: egg layer

Length: 2 to 3½ feet
Home: eastern United States
Order: Lizards and snakes
Family: Anguids

 Grasslands

 Reptiles

© SUZANNE L. & JOSEPH T. COLLINS / PHOTO RESEARCHERS

Glass lizards are named for their fragile tail, which can shatter into pieces like glass. If an enemy attacks the tail, the lizard will likely thrash about, shattering the tail and making escape possible. The name also describes the lizard's glossy body armor.

The slender glass lizard is easily distinguished from its cousins by its slim build and the handsome dark stripes down its back and sides. While some glass lizards have tiny legs, this species has none at all. It is perfectly designed for burrowing and slithering into tight places. Like many burrowing reptiles, the lizard has movable eyelids that protect its eyes from loose dirt. Despite its stiff body armor, the glass lizard can squirm and thrash about violently. Its

flexibility comes from the deep grooves that run along the sides of the body. These lizards are most active during the day, when they slip through the underbrush in search of small creatures such as snails, insects, and other lizards. As a rule the lizard moves slowly. But it can wriggle away quickly when frightened. It often seeks shelter among rocks or in the burrows of small animals.

Mating occurs in May. After the female lays her eggs, she wraps her body around them. For the next two months, she incubates the clutch, leaving only briefly to hunt. When the eggs hatch, the mother guards her babies for a short while before the family scatters.

Smooth-headed Helmeted Lizard
Corytophanes cristatus

Length: up to 14 inches
Number of Eggs: 6 to 11
Home: southern Mexico through Central America to Colombia

Diet: mainly insects and spiders
Order: Lizards and snakes
Family: Iguanas

 Rainforests

 Reptiles

© JOSEPH L. COLLINS / PHOTO RESEARCHERS

The smooth-headed helmeted lizard is a slender iguana with a bold, striped tail about twice the length of its body. This creature is one of three species of helmeted iguanas living in the tropical rainforests of Central America. It is named for the bony crown on the back of its head and neck. Behind this crown, or helmet, is a soft, ridged crest of skin that extends down the lizard's neck and between its shoulders. Males have much larger crests than their mates; both are brown with dark spots and bands.

The helmeted lizard is an excellent climber and seldom descends from the trees. Its enemies include wild cats, birds of prey, and large tropical snakes. And it is hunted by humans, who catch the young to sell as terrarium pets. When attacked, the lizard tries to frighten away its enemy by standing tall on a high branch, raising its crest, and inflating its large throat pouch. The lizard then opens its eyes as wide as possible and stares. Males, which are territorial and quarrelsome, use this same stance when trying to intimidate each other.

In the constant warmth of the tropics, newborn lizards can survive at any time of the year. And breeding occurs year-round. The female lays a clutch of up to 11 eggs in a tree hole or in the crook of a large branch. The newborn look like miniature versions of their parents.

Southern Alligator Lizard
Gerrhonotus multicarinatus

Length: 10 to 16½ inches
Home: northwestern Mexico, California, Oregon, and southern Washington

Diet: insects and small animals
Number of Eggs: about 12
Order: Lizards and snakes
Family: Anguids

  Grasslands

Reptiles

© MARK SMITH / PHOTO RESEARCHERS

The southern alligator lizard has a disgusting, but effective, way of discouraging attack. When grabbed, it not only delivers a sharp bite, it also smears its attacker with a spray of excrement.

Left undisturbed, the southern alligator lizard is a handsome creature, with shiny, bright scales and golden eyes. The dark crossbands on its reddish-brown back give this lizard the look of a miniature alligator.

The southern alligator lizard's skin contains lots of bony armor. This may help it withstand its worst enemy, the hot, drying sun of the Southwest. But the armor also leaves the lizard's body very stiff—so stiff, in fact, that the alligator lizard could not expand to breathe except for a groove of soft scales along each side of its body.

The tail of the southern alligator lizard is considerably longer than the rest of its body. Although the tail is stiff, the lizard can use it to grip small branches as it climbs. These little "alligators" are often seen scrambling through bushes and trees in search of insects and baby birds. On the ground, they hunt scorpions, spiders, and slugs, which they find under fallen leaves.

During summer, the female lizard lays two or three clutches of eggs. This lizard's cousin, the northern alligator lizard, lives in a cooler climate. It keeps its eggs warm inside its body until they hatch.

Wall Lizard
Lacerta muralis

Length: 10 inches
Weight: 7 to 10 ounces
Diet: insects, snails, and worms

Number of Eggs: 2 to 8
Home: Central Europe
Order: Lizards and snakes
Family: Old World lizards

Cities, Towns, and Farms

Reptiles

© HANS REINHARD / BRUCE COLEMAN INC.

Wall lizards are most commonly found in and on the old stone fences that are so common in the countryside of Europe. This species was particularly abundant 100 years ago, when stone walls encircled nearly every European vineyard and farm field. Today the wall lizard has disappeared from much of its range, along with the small country farms and quaint stone walls that were its home. The increased use of insecticides may also be to blame for the wall lizard's decline. These poisons are passed on to the wall lizard in the insects, worms, and snails that it eats.

During April, when wall lizards mate, rival males often fight over territory and females. A typical wall lizard battle begins with a staring match. Each male tries to intimidate the other by lowering his head and puffing out his black-striped throat. Usually the less bold lizard will back down before any biting begins. The victor wins the right to mate with his chosen female. The fertilized female then tucks her eggs into a deep crack in a wall or buries them in the ground. The young hatch sometime in August.

Wall lizards can be good pets that require only a sandy cage, a few rocks, a large water dish, and lots of insects. Perhaps the nicest thing about this pet is that, with the proper care, a wall lizard can live more than 15 years.

Coolie Loach
Acanthophthalmus kuhli kuhli

Length: up to 3½ inches
Method of Reproduction: egg layer
Home: Sumatra, Java, Borneo, Singapore, Thailand, and Malaysia

Diet: plant material, smaller fish, and invertebrates
Order: Carps and their relatives
Family: Loaches

Fresh Water

Fish

© MARK SMITH / PHOTO RESEACHERS

The snakelike coolie loach swims like an eel, undulating its body from side to side. Below its small, toothless mouth dangle several "whiskers," properly called barbels. The loach uses its barbels as feelers to search for food along the soft, sandy bottom of lakes and streams. To the touch, the coolie loach is slick and smooth. It is covered with a protective mucus, or slime. Males and females look very similar, although the female is somewhat fatter, especially during breeding season.

You must look closely to see the coolie loach's tiny eyes. They are located high atop the middle of its head, covered with a thin layer of transparent skin. Below each eye is a stiff, nonpoisonous spine, from which the fish gets its Latin genus name: *Acanthophthalmus,* or "spine-eye." The fish's species name, *kuhli,* as well as its common name, "coolie," are in honor of the German naturalist Heinrich Kuhl.

In the wild, coolie loaches live in small groups. They spawn at the surface of very shallow water. The mating couple presses close together, a behavior called a nuptial embrace. Loaches are popular aquarium fish because they are peaceful scavengers that work hard to keep their tank clean. However, captive loaches remain quite shy. To be happy, they need a shady tank with plenty of hiding places such as empty flower pots and broken coconut shells.

43

Stone Loach
Noemacheilus barbatulus

Length: up to 4½ inches
Diet: worms and insects
Method of Reproduction: egg layer

Home: Europe and Asia
Order: Carps and their relatives
Family: Loaches

Fresh Water

Fish

© HANS REINHARD / BRUCE COLEMAN INC.

The stone loach lives in clean, rapid streams with pebbly bottoms. Occasionally it is also found along the shores of crystal-clear lakes. The creature's name comes from the fish's habit of covering stones and rocks with its large, sticky eggs. Neither parent stays around to guard the eggs, but so many are laid that it doesn't matter that some are eaten by other fish.

Between 8 and 11 days after the eggs are laid, the newborns appear. After the baby fish hatches, it still carries around the yolk sac from its egg, which remains attached to its gut. The yolk supplies the newborn with food for a little more than a week. Then it must begin to hunt for its meals.

As it matures, the stone loach grows three pairs of delicate whiskers, called "barbels," which are very similar to those worn by catfish. These whiskers are actually sense organs. The loach uses them to both smell and feel for worms and insects in the pebbly waterbed.

Like other fish, the stone loach takes oxygen out of the water through its gills. But the loach also comes to the surface to gulp down air. Unlike lungfish, the stone loach does not breathe air into primitive lungs, or swim bladders. It literally swallows air bubbles into its stomach. Some of the oxygen in the bubbles passes through the loach's gut and into its bloodstream.

Set Index

A

adder **1**:5
adder, rhombic night **1**:6
African bat-eared fox **3**:42
African scorpion, giant **8**:16
African snail, giant **8**:37
African twig snake **8**:38
African wild dog **3**:20
agile frog **3**:44
agouti, orange-rumped **1**:7
Alaskan pika (collared pika) **7**:23
Algerian hedgehog **5**:11
alligator lizard, southern **5**:41
alpaca **1**:8
alpine newt **6**:43
American black vulture **10**:24
American crow **3**:8
American tree sparrow **9**:11
amphibians
  caecilian, Ceylonese **2**:10
  frog, agile **3**:44
  frog, burrowing tree **4**:5
  frog, common gray tree **4**:6
  frog, European tree **4**:7
  frog, gold **4**:8
  frog, marbled reed **4**:9
  frog, marsupial **4**:10
  frog, moor **4**:11
  frog, northern chorus **4**:12
  frog, ornate horned **4**:13
  frog, paradox **4**:14
  frog, pickerel **4**:15
  frog, pig **4**:16
  frog, red-legged **4**:17
  frog, strawberry poison dart
    4:18
  newt, alpine **6**:43
  newt, crested (warty) **6**:44
  salamander, common dusky
    8:13
  salamander, fire **8**:14
  spadefoot, European **9**:10
  toad, Eurasian common **9**:42
  toad, green **9**:43
  toad, Surinam **9**:44
anemone, opelet **1**:9
anemone, silver-spotted (gem
  anemone) **1**:10
angel shark, European **8**:22
anoa **1**:11
ant, leaf-cutter **1**:12
anteater, dwarf **1**:13
anteater, scaly (giant pangolin)
  1:14
arctic fulmar **4**:19
arctic hare **5**:7
argus, blue-spotted **1**:15
arrau (giant South American river
  turtle) **10**:14
arthropods **6**:18
  ant, leaf-cutter **1**:12
  backswimmer, common **1**:16
  beetle, cellar **1**:28
  beetle, checkered (bee-wolf)
    1:29
  beetle, European rhinoceros
    1:30
  beetle, forest dung **1**:31
  beetle, whirligig **1**:32
  butterfly, brimstone **2**:7
  butterfly, sail (scarce
    swallowtail) **2**:8
  cockroach, wood **2**:32
  cricket, bush (bush katydid)
    2:44
  cricket, European mole **3**:5
  cricket, Mormon **3**:6
  daphnia (water flea) **3**:37
  darner, blue-green **3**:12
  darner, green **3**:13
  fly, large bee **3**:40
  grasshopper, blue-winged
    wasteland **4**:36
  grasshopper, green valley **4**:37
  hawkmoth, broad-bordered bee
    5:10

horntail, large **5**:17
horsefly, cattle **5**:19
katydid, steppe **5**:26
locust, migratory **6**:5
louse, human-body **6**:7
mosquito, eastern malaria **6**:34
moth, common magpie **6**:35
moth, six-spot burnet **6**:36
prawn, common European
  (palaemon) **7**:33
scorpion, giant African **8**:16
sexton (burying beetle) **8**:20
snakefly **9**:5
spider, goldenrod **9**:14
swallowtail, common
  European **9**:29
tortoiseshell **10**:7
treehopper **10**:9
treehopper, oak **10**:10
white, marbled **10**:36
Atlantic cod **2**:33
Australian lungfish **6**:8
Australian sea lion **8**:17
axis deer (chital) **3**:14
azure-winged magpie **6**:13

B

backswimmer, common **1**:16
Baikal seal **8**:18
Baird's beaked whale **10**:34
bandicoot, large, short-nosed **1**:17
barb, half-banded **1**:18
barbet, crimson-breasted **1**:19
barnacle, common goose **1**:20
barracuda, Pacific **1**:21
basilisk, double-crested **1**:22
bat, Gambian epaulet **1**:23
bat, Honduran white **1**:24
bat, large mouse-eared **1**:25
bat-eared fox, African **3**:42
beaked whale, Baird's **10**:34
bear, sloth **1**:26
bearded vulture **10**:25
beaver, Eurasian **1**:27
bee fly, large **3**:40
bee hawkmoth, broad-bordered
  5:10
beetle, burying (sexton) **8**:20
beetle, cellar **1**:28
beetle, checkered (bee-wolf) **1**:29
beetle, European rhinoceros **1**:30
beetle, forest dung **1**:31
beetle, whirligig **1**:32
bee-wolf (checkered beetle) **1**:29
bird of paradise, greater **1**:33
birds
  barbet, crimson-breasted **1**:19
  bird of paradise, greater **1**:33
  bittern, Eurasian **1**:35
  bluebird, blue-backed fairy
    1:37
  booby, blue-footed **1**:38
  booby, brown **1**:39
  bower-bird, satin **1**:40
  bunting, corn **2**:5
  chickadee, black-capped **2**:23
  chicken, greater prairie **2**:24
  courser, cream-colored **2**:43
  crossbill, red **3**:7
  crow, American **3**:8
  crow, carrion **3**:9
  crow, fish **3**:10
  dove, laughing **3**:24
  duck, torrent **3**:26
  dunlin **3**:27
  eagle, tawny **3**:30
  finch, snow **3**:36
  flicker, red-shafted **3**:38
  flycatcher, fork-tailed **3**:41
  fulmar, arctic **4**:19
  goose, magpie **4**:33
  greenfinch **4**:38
  greenshank **4**:39
  grouse, double-banded sand
    4:40
  gull, great black-backed **5**:5

heron, little blue **5**:12
heron, nankeen night **5**:13
heron, purple **5**:14
hornbill, red-billed **5**:16
jacamar, rufous-tailed **5**:21
jacana, wattled **5**:22
lapwing **5**:31
lorikeet, musk **6**:6
macaw, blue-and-yellow **6**:11
macaw, military **6**:12
magpie, azure-winged **6**:13
manakin, red-capped **6**:15
martin, sand **6**:17
merganser, red-breasted **6**:19
nuthatch, Eurasian **7**:5
owl, great gray **7**:8
owl, scops **7**:9
owl, short-eared **7**:10
owl, tawny **7**:11
parakeet, rose-ringed **7**:13
parrot, king **7**:14
penguin, Galápagos **7**:16
penguin, gentoo **7**:17
petrel, southern giant **7**:19
pheasant, Reeve's **7**:20
pipit, water **7**:24
plover, spur-winged **7**:26
pochard, red-crested **7**:27
puffin, tufted **7**:35
quail, little button **7**:40
quetzal **7**:41
roller, common **8**:9
roller, lilac-breasted **8**:10
sandpiper, wood **8**:15
shag, imperial **8**:21
shelduck, common **8**:26
siskin, Eurasian **8**:30
sparrow, American tree **9**:11
sparrow, hedge **9**:12
sparrow, Java **9**:13
starling, superb **9**:22
stonechat **9**:24
stork, white **9**:25
swan, whooper **9**:30
tanager, scarlet **9**:33
tern, whiskered **9**:37
thrush, mistle **9**:40
thrush, rock **9**:41
toucan, keel-billed **10**:8
vireo, white-eyed **10**:21
vulture, American black **10**:24
vulture, bearded **10**:25
vulture, king **10**:26
vulture, lappet-faced **10**:27
wagtail, white **10**:28
wagtail, yellow **10**:29
waxbill, red-cheeked (cordon-
  bleu) **10**:30
waxwing, cedar **10**:31
weaver, grenadier (red bishop)
  10:32
whydah, pin-tailed **10**:37
wren, superb blue **10**:43
bishop, red (grenadier weaver)
  10:32
bitterling **1**:34
bittern, Eurasian **1**:35
black-backed gull, great **5**:5
black-backed jackal **5**:23
blackbuck **1**:36
black-capped chickadee **2**:23
black mamba **6**:14
black ruby **8**:11
black vulture, American **10**:24
bleeding-heart tetra **9**:38
blind cavefish **2**:20
blue-and-yellow macaw **6**:11
blue-backed fairy bluebird **1**:37
bluebird, blue-backed fairy **1**:37
blue-footed booby **1**:38
blue-green darner **3**:12
blue heron, little **5**:12
blue-spotted argus **1**:15
blue stentor **9**:23
blue-tailed day gecko **4**:24
blue-winged wasteland
  grasshopper **4**:36

blue wren, superb **10**:43
booby, blue-footed **1**:38
booby, brown **1**:39
bower-bird, satin **1**:40
bowfin **1**:41
bream, common **1**:42
brimstone butterfly **2**:7
broad-bordered bee hawkmoth
  5:10
brocket, red **1**:43
bronze catfish **2**:16
brown booby **1**:39
brush-tailed possum **7**:31
buffalo, water **1**:44
bunting, corn **2**:5
burnet moth, six-spot **6**:36
burrowing tree frog **4**:5
burying beetle (sexton) **8**:20
bushbuck **2**:6
bush cricket (bush katydid) **2**:44
butterfly, brimstone **2**:7
butterfly, sail (scarce swallowtail)
  2:8
butterflyfish, freshwater **2**:9
button quail, little **7**:40

C

caecilian, Ceylonese **2**:10
California legless lizard **5**:33
Cape girdled lizard, common
  5:34
Cape hyrax **5**:20
Cape monitor **6**:26
caribou (reindeer) **8**:7
carp, common **2**:11
carpet python **7**:36
carpet shell, crosscut **8**:27
carrion crow **3**:9
cat, European wild **2**:12
cat, Geoffroy's **2**:13
cat, Iriomote **2**:14
cat, ring-tailed **2**:15
catfish, bronze **2**:16
catfish, Congo **2**:17
catfish, glass **2**:18
catfish, shovelnose **2**:19
cat tapeworm **9**:34
cavefish, blind **2**:20
cedar waxwing **10**:31
cellar beetle **1**:28
Ceylonese caecilian **2**:10
chamois **2**:21
checkered beetle (bee-wolf) **1**:29
chevrotain, water **2**:22
chickadee, black-capped **2**:23
chicken, greater prairie **2**:24
Chinese water deer **3**:15
chital (axis deer) **3**:14
chorus frog, northern **4**:12
chub **2**:25
chuckwalla **2**:26
cichlid, firemouth **2**:27
cichlid, lionhead **2**:28
civet, masked palm **2**:29
coati, ring-tailed **2**:30
cobra, king **2**:31
cockroach, wood **2**:32
cod, Atlantic **2**:33
coelacanth **2**:34
collared pika (Alaskan pika) **7**:23
colpeo fox **3**:43
column sponge, purple **9**:16
common backswimmer **1**:16
common bream **1**:42
common Cape girdled lizard **5**:34
common carp **2**:11
common dusky salamander **8**:13
common European prawn
  (palaemon) **7**:33
common European swallowtail
  9:29
common goose barnacle **1**:20
common goral **4**:34
common gray tree frog **4**:6
common gudgeon **4**:42

common langur **5**:30
common liver fluke **3**:39
common magpie moth **6**:35
common piddock **7**:21
common porpoise **7**:30
common roller **8**:9
common shelduck **8**:26
common shrew, Eurasian **8**:29
common toad, Eurasian **9**:42
common tree shrew **8**:28
conch, rooster-tail **2**:35
conger eel **3**:32
Congo catfish **2**:17
coolie loach **5**:43
coral, Devonshire cup **2**:36
coral, large star **2**:37
coral, northern stony **2**:38
coral, red precious **2**:39
coral, staghorn **2**:40
coral, star **2**:41
cordon-bleu (red-cheeked)
    waxbill **10**:30
corn bunting **2**:5
corn snake **8**:39
cottontail, New England **2**:42
courser, cream-colored **2**:43
crab-eating macaque **6**:9
cream-colored courser **2**:43
crested (warty) newt **6**:44
cricket, bush (bush katydid) **2**:44
cricket, European mole **3**:5
cricket, Mormon **3**:6
crimson-breasted barbet **1**:19
crossbill, red **3**:7
crosscut carpet shell **8**:27
crow, American **3**:8
crow, carrion **3**:9
crow, fish **3**:10
cup coral, Devonshire **2**:36

D

daboia (Russell's viper) **10**:20
dace **3**:11
daphnia (water flea) **3**:37
dark-green racer **7**:43
darner, blue-green **3**:12
darner, green **3**:13
deer, axis (chital) **3**:14
deer, Chinese water **3**:15
deer, fallow **3**:16
deer, pampas **3**:17
deer, red **3**:18
desert monitor **6**:27
Devonshire cup coral **2**:36
dhaman **3**:19
dog, African wild **3**:20
dogfish, spiny **3**:21
dollar, eccentric sand **3**:22
dolphin, Pacific white-sided **3**:23
dorcas gazelle **4**:23
Dory, European John **5**:25
double-banded sand grouse **4**:40
double-crested basilisk **1**:22
dove, laughing **3**:24
duck, torrent **3**:26
dung beetle, forest **1**:31
dunlin **3**:27
dusky salamander, common **8**:13
duster, magnificent feather **3**:28
duster, slime feather **3**:29
dwarf anteater **1**:13
dwarf mongoose **6**:24

E

eagle, tawny **3**:30
eastern malaria mosquito **6**:34
eccentric sand dollar **3**:22
echidna, long-nosed **3**:31
eel, conger **3**:32
Egyptian spiny mouse **6**:38
elephant, forest **3**:33
endangered animals
    anoa **1**:11
    cat, Iriomote **2**:14
    chamois **2**:21
    deer, pampas **3**:17
    dog, African wild **3**:20
    elephant, forest **3**:33
    gavial **4**:21
    gazelle, gazelle **4**:23

goat, wild **4**:32
guemal, Peruvian **4**:44
hog, pygmy **5**:15
horse, Przewalski's **5**:18
langur, common **5**:30
lemur, gentle gray **5**:32
moloch (silvery gibbon) **4**:28
monitor, desert **6**:27
monkey, Goeldi's **6**:30
monkey, woolly spider
    (muriqui) **6**:32
penguin, Galápagos **7**:16
pronghorn **7**:34
quetzal **7**:41
solenodon, Haitian **9**:8
stork, white **9**:25
turtle, giant South American
    river (arrau) **10**:14
epaulet bat, Gambian **1**:23
Eurasian beaver **1**:27
Eurasian bittern **1**:35
Eurasian common shrew **8**:29
Eurasian common toad **9**:42
Eurasian minnow **6**:21
Eurasian nuthatch **7**:5
Eurasian siskin **8**:30
European mink **6**:20
European mole **6**:22
European mole cricket **3**:5
European mouflon **6**:37
European perch **7**:18
European prawn, common
    (palaemon) **7**:33
European rhinoceros beetle **1**:30
European sole **9**:7
European spadefoot **9**:10
European swallowtail, common
    9:29
European tree frog **4**:7
European water vole **10**:23
European wild cat **2**:12
European wild rabbit **7**:42

F

fairy bluebird, blue-backed **1**:37
fallow deer **3**:16
false gavial **4**:22
feather duster, magnificent **3**:28
feather duster, slime **3**:29
featherworm, peacock **3**:34
filefish, orange-spotted **3**:35
finch, snow **3**:36
firemouth cichlid **2**:27
fire salamander **8**:14
fire sponge **9**:15
fish
    argus, blue-spotted **1**:15
    barb, half-banded **1**:18
    barracuda, Pacific **1**:21
    bitterling **1**:34
    bowfin **1**:41
    bream, common **1**:42
    butterflyfish, freshwater **2**:9
    carp, common **2**:11
    catfish, bronze **2**:16
    catfish, Congo **2**:17
    catfish, glass **2**:18
    catfish, shovelnose **2**:19
    cavefish, blind **2**:20
    chub **2**:25
    cichlid, firemouth **2**:27
    cichlid, lionhead **2**:28
    cod, Atlantic **2**:33
    coelacanth **2**:34
    dace **3**:11
    dogfish, spiny **3**:21
    eel, conger **3**:32
    filefish, orange-spotted **3**:35
    gourami, striped **4**:35
    gudgeon, common **4**:42
    John Dory, European **5**:25
    loach, coolie **5**:43
    loach, stone **5**:44
    lungfish, Australian **6**:8
    minnow, Eurasian **6**:21
    perch, European **7**:18
    piranha, white **7**:25
    redfish **8**:6
    roach **8**:8
    ruby, black **8**:11

rudd **8**:12
shark, European angel **8**:22
shark, great hammerhead **8**:23
shark, Port Jackson **8**:24
sharksucker **8**:25
smelt, sand **8**:36
snipefish, longspine **9**:6
sole, European **9**:7
spadefish **9**:9
surgeonfish, powder-blue
    surgeon **9**:27
swordtail **9**:31
tetra, bleeding-heart **9**:38
tetra, glowlight **9**:39
triggerfish, redtooth **10**:11
triggerfish, undulate **10**:12
turbot **10**:13
unicornfish **10**:17
wels **10**:33
fish crow **3**:10
fishing (tentacled) snake **8**:44
flea, water (daphnia) **3**:37
flicker, red-shafted **3**:38
fluke, common liver **3**:39
fly, large bee **3**:40
flycatcher, fork-tailed **3**:41
flying possum, pygmy **7**:32
forest dung beetle **1**:31
forest elephant **3**:33
forest pig, giant **7**:22
fork-tailed flycatcher **3**:41
fox, African bat-eared **3**:42
fox, colpeo **3**:43
freshwater butterflyfish **2**:9
frog, agile **3**:44
frog, burrowing tree **4**:5
frog, common gray tree **4**:6
frog, European tree **4**:7
frog, gold **4**:8
frog, marbled reed **4**:9
frog, marsupial **4**:10
frog, moor **4**:11
frog, northern chorus **4**:12
frog, ornate horned **4**:13
frog, paradox **4**:14
frog, pickerel **4**:15
frog, pig **4**:16
frog, red-legged **4**:17
frog, strawberry poison dart **4**:18
fulmar, arctic **4**:19
fur seal, South American **8**:19

G

Gaboon viper **10**:19
Galápagos penguin **7**:16
Gambian epaulet bat **1**:23
gaur **4**:20
gavial **4**:21
gavial, false **4**:22
gazelle, dorcas **4**:23
gecko, blue-tailed day **4**:24
gecko, gliding **4**:25
gecko, Madagascar **4**:26
gecko, northern leaf-tailed **4**:27
gem anemone **1**:10
gentle gray lemur **5**:32
gentoo penguin **7**:17
Geoffroy's cat **2**:13
giant African scorpion **8**:16
giant African snail **8**:37
giant forest pig **7**:22
giant pangolin (scaly anteater)
    1:14
giant petrel, southern **7**:19
giant South American river turtle
    (arrau) **10**:14
giant tube sponge **9**:16
gibbon, silvery (moloch) **4**:28
gibbon, white-cheeked **4**:29
Gila monster **6**:33
giraffe, reticulated **4**:30
girdled lizard, common Cape
    5:34
glass catfish **2**:18
glass lizard, slender **5**:39
glider, yellow-bellied **4**:31
gliding gecko **4**:25
glowlight tetra **9**:39
goat, wild **4**:32
Goeldi's monkey **6**:30

golden-mantled ground squirrel
    9:20
goldenrod spider **9**:14
gold frog **4**:8
goose, magpie **4**:33
goose barnacle, common **1**:20
gopher snake **8**:40
gopher tortoise **10**:5
goral, common **4**:34
Gould's monitor **6**:28
gourami, striped **4**:35
grasshopper, blue-winged
    wasteland **4**:36
grasshopper, green valley **4**:37
grass snake **8**:41
gray lemur, gentle **5**:32
gray tree frog, common **4**:6
great black-backed gull **5**:5
greater bird of paradise **1**:33
greater kudu **5**:28
greater prairie chicken **2**:24
great gray owl **7**:8
great hammerhead shark **8**:22
green darner **3**:13
greenfinch **4**:38
greenshank **4**:39
green toad **9**:43
green tree python **7**:37
green valley grasshopper **4**:37
grenadier weaver (red bishop)
    10:32
grivet (savanna monkey) **6**:31
ground squirrel, golden-mantled
    9:20
grouse, double-banded sand **4**:40
guanaco **4**:41
gudgeon, common **4**:42
guemal, Peruvian **4**:44
guenon, moustached **4**:43
gull, great black-backed **5**:5

H

Haitian solenodon **9**:8
half-banded barb **1**:18
hammerhead shark, great **8**:23
hardun **5**:6
hare, arctic **5**:7
hartebeest **5**:8
hartebeest, hunter's (hirola) **5**:9
hawkmoth, broad-bordered bee
    5:10
hedgehog, Algerian **5**:11
hedgehog tenrec, lesser **9**:36
hedge sparrow **9**:12
helmeted lizard, smooth-headed
    5:40
helmeted turtle **10**:15
heron, little blue **5**:12
heron, purple **5**:14
Himalayan tahr **9**:32
hirola (hunter's hartebeest) **5**:9
Hoffmann's two-toed sloth **8**:33
hog, pygmy **5**:15
Honduran white bat **1**:24
hornbill, red-billed **5**:16
horned frog, ornate **4**:13
horntail, large **5**:17
horse, Przewalski's **5**:18
horsefly, cattle **5**:19
horsehair worm **10**:39
human-body louse **6**:7
hunter's hartebeest (hirola) **5**:9
hyrax, Cape **5**:20

I

ice cream cone worm **10**:40
imperial shag **8**:21
invertebrates, other
    anemone, opelet **1**:9
    anemone, silver-spotted (gem
        anemone) **1**:10
    barnacle, common goose **1**:20
    conch, rooster-tail **2**:35
    coral, Devonshire cup **2**:36
    coral, large star **2**:37
    coral, northern stony **2**:38
    coral, red precious **2**:39
    coral, staghorn **2**:40
    coral, star **2**:41
    dollar, eccentric sand **3**:22

duster, magnificent feather **3**:28
duster, slime feather **3**:29
featherworm, peacock **3**:34
fluke, common liver **3**:39
jellyfish, trumpet-stalked (stauromedusan) **5**:24
mussel, swan **6**:40
nettle, sea **6**:42
orange, sea **7**:7
paw, kitten's **7**:15
piddock, common **7**:21
razor, pod **7**:44
shell, crosscut carpet **8**:27
slug, red **8**:35
snail, giant African **8**:37
sponge, fire **9**:15
sponge, purple column (giant tube) **9**:16
sponge, stinker **9**:17
sponge, vase **9**:18
star, slime **9**:21
stentor, blue **9**:23
tapeworm, cat **9**:34
urchin, slate-pencil **10**:18
whelk, waved **10**:35
worm, horsehair **10**:39
worm, ice cream cone **10**:40
worm, peripatus velvet **10**:41
worm, red tube **10**:42
Iriomote cat **2**:14
Italian wall lizard **5**:35

J-K

jacamar, rufous-tailed **5**:21
jacana, wattled **5**:22
jackal, black-backed **5**:23
Japanese macaque **6**:10
Java sparrow **9**:13
jellyfish, trumpet-stalked (stauromedusan) **5**:24
John Dory, European **5**:25
katydid, bush (bush cricket) **2**:44
katydid, steppe **5**:26
keel-billed toucan **10**:8
king cobra **2**:31
king parrot **7**:14
kingsnake, prairie **5**:27
king vulture **10**:26
kitten's paw **7**:15
kudu, greater **5**:28
kudu, lesser **5**:29

L

langur, common **5**:30
lappet-faced vulture **10**:27
lapwing **5**:31
large, short-nosed bandicoot **1**:17
large bee fly **3**:40
large horntail **5**:17
large mouse-eared bat **1**:25
large star coral **2**:37
laughing dove **3**:24
leaf-cutter ant **1**:12
leaf-tailed gecko, northern **4**:27
legless lizard, California **5**:33
lemur, gentle gray **5**:32
lesser hedgehog tenrec **9**:36
lesser kudu **5**:29
lilac-breasted roller **8**:10
lionhead cichlid **2**:28
little blue heron **5**:12
little button quail **7**:40
liver fluke, common **3**:39
lizard, California legless **5**:33
lizard, common Cape girdled **5**:34
lizard, Italian wall **5**:35
lizard, lyre-headed **5**:36
lizard, sand **5**:37
lizard, short-horned **5**:38
lizard, slender glass **5**:39
lizard, smooth-headed helmeted **5**:40
lizard, southern alligator **5**:41
lizard, wall **5**:42
loach, coolie **5**:43
loach, stone **5**:44
locust, migratory **6**:5
long-nosed echidna **3**:31

longspine snipefish **9**:6
lorikeet, musk **6**:6
louse, human-body **6**:7
lungfish, Australian **6**:8
lyre-headed lizard **5**:36

M

macaque, crab-eating **6**:9
macaque, Japanese **6**:10
macaw, blue-and-yellow **6**:11
macaw, military **6**:12
Madagascar gecko **4**:26
magnificent feather duster **3**:28
magpie, azure-winged **6**:13
magpie goose **4**:33
magpie moth, common **6**:35
malaria mosquito, eastern **6**:34
mamba, black **6**:14
mammals
  agouti, orange-rumped **1**:7
  alpaca **1**:8
  anoa **1**:11
  anteater, dwarf **1**:13
  anteater, scaly (giant pangolin) **1**:14
  bandicoot, large, short-nosed **1**:17
  bat, Gambian epaulet **1**:23
  bat, Honduran white **1**:24
  bat, large mouse-eared **1**:25
  bear, sloth **1**:26
  beaver, Eurasian **1**:27
  blackbuck **1**:36
  brocket, red **1**:43
  buffalo, water **1**:44
  bushbuck **2**:6
  cat, European wild **2**:12
  cat, Geoffroy's **2**:13
  cat, Iriomote **2**:14
  cat, ring-tailed **2**:15
  chamois **2**:21
  chevrotain, water **2**:22
  civet, masked palm **2**:29
  coati, ring-tailed **2**:30
  cottontail, New England **2**:42
  deer, axis (chital) **3**:14
  deer, Chinese water **3**:15
  deer, fallow **3**:16
  deer, pampas **3**:17
  deer, red **3**:18
  dog, African wild **3**:20
  dolphin, Pacific white-sided **3**:23
  echidna, long-nosed **3**:31
  elephant, forest **3**:33
  fox, African bat-eared **3**:42
  fox, colpeo **3**:43
  gaur **4**:20
  gazelle, dorcas **4**:23
  gibbon, silvery (moloch) **4**:28
  gibbon, white-cheeked **4**:29
  giraffe, reticulated **4**:30
  glider, yellow-bellied **4**:31
  goat, wild **4**:32
  goral, common **4**:34
  guanaco **4**:41
  guemal, Peruvian **4**:44
  guenon, moustached **4**:43
  hare, arctic **5**:7
  hartebeest **5**:8
  hedgehog, Algerian **5**:11
  hirola (hunter's hartebeest) **5**:9
  hog, pygmy **5**:15
  horse, Przewalski's **5**:18
  hyrax, Cape **5**:20
  jackal, black-backed **5**:23
  kudu, greater **5**:28
  kudu, lesser **5**:29
  langur, common **5**:30
  lemur, gentle gray **5**:32
  macaque, crab-eating **6**:9
  macaque, Japanese **6**:10
  marmot, Olympic **6**:16
  mink, European **6**:20
  mole, European **6**:22
  mongoose, mongoose **6**:24
  mongoose, white-tailed **6**:25
  monkey, Goeldi's **6**:30
  monkey, savanna (grivet) **6**:31

monkey, woolly spider (muriqui) **6**:32
mouflon, European **6**:37
mouse, Egyptian spiny **6**:38
mouse, wood **6**:39
narwhal **6**:41
olingo **7**:6
pademelon, red-legged **7**:12
pig, giant forest **7**:22
pika, collared (Alaskan pika) **7**:23
polecat, striped (zorilla) **7**:28
porcupine, tree **7**:29
porpoise, common **7**:30
possum, brush-tailed **7**:31
possum, pygmy flying **7**:32
pronghorn **7**:34
rabbit, European wild **7**:42
reedbuck, mountain **8**:5
reindeer (caribou) **8**:7
seal, Baikal **8**:18
seal, South American fur **8**:19
sea lion, Australian **8**:17
shrew, common tree **8**:28
shrew, Eurasian common **8**:29
sloth, Hoffmann's two-toed **8**:33
sloth, three-toed **8**:34
solenodon, Haitian **9**:8
springbok **9**:19
squirrel, golden-mantled ground **9**:20
suricate (meerkat) **9**:28
tahr, Himalayan **9**:32
tarsier, western **9**:35
tenrec, lesser hedgehog **9**:36
viscacha, plains **10**:22
vole, European water **10**:23
whale, Baird's beaked **10**:34
wolf, maned **10**:38
zebu **10**:44
manakin, red-capped **6**:15
maned wolf **10**:38
marbled reed frog **4**:9
marbled white **10**:36
marmot, Olympic **6**:16
marsupial frog **4**:10
martin, sand **6**:17
masked palm civet **2**:29
Mediterranean tortoise, spur-tailed **10**:6
meerkat (suricate) **9**:28
merganser, red-breasted **6**:19
migratory locust **6**:5
military macaw **6**:12
mink, European **6**:20
minnow, Eurasian **6**:21
mistle thrush **9**:40
mole, European **6**:22
mole cricket, European **3**:5
moloch (lizard) **6**:23
moloch (silvery gibbon) **4**:28
mongoose, dwarf **6**:24
mongoose, white-tailed **6**:25
monitor, Cape **6**:26
monitor, desert **6**:27
monitor, Gould's **6**:28
monitor, Nile **6**:29
monkey, Goeldi's **6**:30
monkey, savanna (grivet) **6**:31
monkey, woolly spider (muriqui) **6**:32
moor frog **4**:11
Mormon cricket **3**:6
mosquito, eastern malaria **6**:34
moth, common magpie **6**:35
moth, six-spot burnet **6**:36
mouflon, European **6**:37
mountain reedbuck **8**:5
mouse, Egyptian spiny **6**:38
mouse, wood **6**:39
mouse-eared bat, large **1**:25
moustached guenon **4**:43
muriqui (woolly spider monkey) **6**:32
musk lorikeet **6**:6
mussel, swan **6**:40

N

nankeen night heron **5**:13

narwhal **6**:41
New England cottontail **2**:42
newt, alpine **6**:43
newt, crested (warty) **6**:44
night heron, nankeen **5**:13
Nile monitor **6**:29
northern chorus frog **4**:12
northern leaf-tailed gecko **4**:27
northern stony coral **2**:38
nuthatch, Eurasian **7**:5

O

oak treehopper **10**:10
olingo **7**:6
Olympic marmot **6**:16
opelet anemone **1**:9
orange-rumped agouti **1**:7
orange-spotted filefish **3**:35
oriental beauty snake **8**:42
oriental water dragon **3**:25
ornate horned frog **4**:13
owl, great gray **7**:8
owl, scops **7**:9
owl, short-eared **7**:10
owl, tawny **7**:11

P

Pacific barracuda **1**:21
Pacific white-sided dolphin **3**:23
pademelon, red-legged **7**:12
palaemon (common European prawn) **7**:33
palm civet, masked **2**:29
pampas deer **3**:17
pangolin, giant (scaly anteater) **1**:14
paradox frog **4**:14
parakeet, rose-ringed **7**:13
parrot, king **7**:14
peacock featherworm **3**:34
penguin, Galápagos **7**:16
penguin, gentoo **7**:17
perch, European **7**:18
peripatus velvet worm **10**:41
Peruvian guemal **4**:44
petrel, southern giant **7**:19
pheasant, Reeve's **7**:20
pickerel frog **4**:15
piddock, common **7**:21
pig, giant forest **7**:22
pig frog **4**:16
pika, collared (Alaskan pika) **7**:23
pin-tailed whydah **10**:37
pipe snake, red-tailed **8**:43
pipit, water **7**:24
piranha, white **7**:25
plains viscacha **10**:22
plover, spur-winged **7**:26
pochard, red-crested **7**:27
pod razor **7**:44
poison dart frog, strawberry **4**:18
polecat, striped (zorilla) **7**:28
porcupine, tree **7**:29
porpoise, common **7**:30
Port Jackson shark **8**:24
possum, brush-tailed **7**:31
possum, pygmy flying **7**:32
powder-blue surgeonfish **9**:27
prairie chicken, greater **2**:24
prairie kingsnake **5**:27
prawn, common European (palaemon) **7**:33
precious coral, red **2**:39
pronghorn **7**:34
Przewalski's horse **5**:18
puffin, tufted **7**:35
purple column sponge **9**:16
purple heron **5**:14
pygmy flying possum **7**:32
pygmy hog **5**:15
python, carpet **7**:36
python, green tree **7**:37
python, reticulate **7**:38
python, rock **7**:39

Q-R

quail, little button **7**:40
quetzal **7**:41

rabbit, European wild **7**:42
racer, dark-green **7**:43
razor, pod **7**:44
red-billed hornbill **5**:16
red bishop (grenadier weaver) **10**:32
red-breasted merganser **6**:19
red brocket **1**:43
red-capped manakin **6**:15
red-cheeked (cordon-bleu) waxbill **10**:30
red-crested pochard **7**:27
red crossbill **3**:7
red deer **3**:18
red-legged frog **4**:17
red-legged pademelon **7**:12
red precious coral **2**:39
red-shafted flicker **3**:38
red slug **8**:35
red-tailed pipe snake **8**:43
redtooth triggerfish **10**:11
red tube worm **10**:42
reedbuck, mountain **8**:5
reedfish **8**:6
reed frog, marbled **4**:9
Reeve's pheasant **7**:20
reindeer (caribou) **8**:7
reptiles
  adder **1**:5
  adder, rhombic night **1**:6
  basilisk, double-crested **1**:22
  chuckwalla **2**:26
  cobra, king **2**:31
  dhaman **3**:19
  dragon, oriental water **3**:25
  gavial **4**:21
  gavial, false **4**:22
  gecko, blue-tailed day **4**:24
  gecko, gliding **4**:25
  gecko, Madagascar **4**:26
  gecko, northern leaf-tailed **4**:27
  hardun **5**:6
  kingsnake, prairie **5**:27
  lizard, California legless **5**:33
  lizard, common Cape girdled **5**:34
  lizard, Italian wall **5**:35
  lizard, lizard **5**:37
  lizard, lyre-headed **5**:36
  lizard, short-horned **5**:38
  lizard, slender glass **5**:39
  lizard, smooth-headed helmeted **5**:40
  lizard, southern alligator **5**:41
  lizard, wall **5**:42
  mamba, black **6**:14
  moloch (lizard) **6**:23
  monitor, Cape **6**:26
  monitor, desert **6**:27
  monitor, Gould's **6**:28
  monitor, Nile **6**:29
  monster, Gila **6**:33
  python, carpet **7**:36
  python, green tree **7**:37
  python, reticulate **7**:38
  python, rock **7**:39
  racer, dark-green **7**:43
  skink, sand **8**:31
  skink, stump-tailed **8**:32
  snake, African twig **8**:38
  snake, corn **8**:39
  snake, gopher **8**:40
  snake, grass **8**:41
  snake, oriental beauty **8**:42
  snake, red-tailed pipe **8**:43
  snake, tentacled (fishing) **8**:44
  sungazer **9**:26
  tortoise, gopher **10**:5
  tortoise, spur-tailed Mediterranean **10**:6
  turtle, giant South American river (arrau) **10**:14
  turtle, helmeted **10**:15
  turtle, spotted **10**:16
  viper, Gaboon **10**:19
  viper, Russell's (daboia) **10**:20
reticulated giraffe **4**:30
reticulated python **7**:38
rhinoceros beetle, European **1**:30

rhombic night adder **1**:6
ring-tailed cat **2**:15
ring-tailed coati **2**:30
river turtle, giant South American (arrau) **10**:14
roach **8**:8
rock python **7**:39
rock thrush **9**:41
roller, common **8**:9
roller, lilac-breasted **8**:10
rooster-tail conch **2**:35
rose-ringed parakeet **7**:13
ruby, black **8**:11
rudd **8**:12
rufous-tailed jacamar **5**:21
Russell's viper (daboia) **10**:20

S

sail butterfly (scarce swallowtail) **2**:8
salamander, common dusky **8**:13
salamander, fire **8**:14
sand dollar, eccentric **3**:22
sand grouse, double-banded **4**:40
sand lizard **5**:37
sand martin **6**:17
sandpiper, wood **8**:15
sand skink **8**:31
sand smelt **8**:36
satin bower-bird **1**:40
savanna monkey (grivet) **6**:31
scaly anteater (giant pangolin) **1**:14
scarce swallowtail (sail butterfly) **2**:8
scarlet tanager **9**:33
scops owl **7**:9
scorpion, giant African **8**:16
seal, Baikal **8**:18
seal, South American fur **8**:19
sea lion, Australian **8**:17
sea nettle **6**:42
sea orange **7**:7
sexton (burying beetle) **8**:20
shag, imperial **8**:21
shark, European angel **8**:22
shark, great hammerhead **8**:23
shark, Port Jackson **8**:24
sharksucker **8**:25
shelduck, common **8**:26
shell, crosscut carpet **8**:27
short-eared owl **7**:10
short-horned lizard **5**:38
short-nosed bandicoot, large **1**:17
shovelnose catfish **2**:19
shrew, common tree **8**:28
shrew, Eurasian common **8**:29
silver-spotted anemone (gem anemone) **1**:10
silvery gibbon (moloch) **4**:28
sink, sand **8**:31
siskin, Eurasian **8**:30
six-spot burnet moth **6**:36
skink, stump-tailed **8**:32
slate-pencil urchin **10**:18
slender glass lizard **5**:39
slime feather duster **3**:29
slime star **9**:21
sloth, Hoffmann's two-toed **8**:33
sloth, three-toed **8**:34
sloth bear **1**:26
slug, red **8**:35
smelt, sand **8**:36
smooth-headed helmeted lizard **5**:40
snail, giant African **8**:37
snake, African twig **8**:38
snake, corn **8**:39
snake, fishing (tentacled) **8**:44
snake, gopher **8**:40
snake, grass **8**:41
snake, oriental beauty **8**:42
snake, red-tailed pipe **8**:43
snakefly **9**:5
snipefish, longspine **9**:6
snow finch **3**:36
sole, European **9**:7
solenodon, Haitian **9**:8
South American fur seal **8**:19

South American river turtle, giant (arrau) **10**:14
southern alligator lizard **5**:41
southern giant petrel **7**:19
spadefish **9**:9
spadefoot, European **9**:10
sparrow, hedge **9**:12
sparrow, Java **9**:13
spider, goldenrod **9**:14
spider monkey, woolly (muriqui) **6**:32
spiny dogfish **3**:21
spiny mouse, Egyptian **6**:38
sponge, fire **9**:15
sponge, purple column (giant tube) **9**:16
sponge, stinker **9**:17
sponge, vase **9**:18
spotted turtle **10**:16
springbok **9**:19
spur-tailed Mediterranean tortoise **10**:6
spur-winged plover **7**:26
squirrel, golden-mantled ground **9**:20
staghorn coral **2**:40
star, slime **9**:21
star coral **2**:41
star coral, large **2**:37
starling, superb **9**:22
stauromedusan (trumpet-stalked jellyfish) **5**:24
stentor, blue **9**:23
steppe katydid **5**:26
stinker sponge **9**:17
stonechat **9**:24
stone loach **5**:44
stony coral, northern **2**:38
stork, white **9**:25
strawberry poison dart frog **4**:18
striped gourami **4**:35
striped polecat (zorilla) **7**:28
stump-tailed skink **8**:32
sungazer **9**:26
superb blue wren **10**:43
superb starling **9**:22
surgeonfish, powder-blue **9**:27
suricate (meerkat) **9**:28
Surinam toad **9**:44
swallowtail, common European **9**:29
swallowtail, scarce (sail butterfly) **2**:8
swan, whooper **9**:30
swan mussel **6**:40
swordtail **9**:31

T

tahr, Himalayan **9**:32
tanager, scarlet **9**:33
tapeworm, cat **9**:34
tarsier, western **9**:35
tawny eagle **3**:30
tawny owl **7**:11
tenrec, lesser hedgehog **9**:36
tentacled (fishing) snake **8**:44
tern, whiskered **9**:37
tetra, bleeding-heart **9**:38
tetra, glowlight **9**:39
three-toed sloth **8**:34
thrush, mistle **9**:40
thrush, rock **9**:41
toad, Eurasian common **9**:42
toad, green **9**:43
toad, Surinam **9**:44
torrent duck **3**:26
tortoise, gopher **10**:5
tortoise, spur-tailed Mediterranean **10**:6
tortoiseshell **10**:7
toucan, keel-billed **10**:8
tree frog, burrowing **4**:5
tree frog, common gray **4**:6
tree frog, European **4**:7
treehopper **10**:9
treehopper, oak **10**:10
tree porcupine **7**:29
tree shrew, common **8**:28
tree sparrow, American tree **9**:11

triggerfish, redtooth **10**:11
triggerfish, undulate **10**:12
trumpet-stalked jellyfish (stauromedusan) **5**:24
tube sponge, giant **9**:16
tube worm, red **10**:42
tufted puffin **7**:35
turbot **10**:13
turtle, giant South American river (arrau) **10**:14
turtle, helmeted **10**:15
turtle, spotted **10**:16
twig snake, African **8**:38
two-toed sloth, Hoffmann's **8**:33

U-V

undulate triggerfish **10**:12
unicornfish **10**:17
urchin, slate-pencil **10**:18
vase sponge **9**:18
velvet worm, peripatus **10**:41
viper, Gaboon **10**:19
viper, Russell's (daboia) **10**:20
vireo, white-eyed **10**:21
viscacha, plains **10**:22
vole, European water **10**:23
vulture, American black **10**:24
vulture, bearded **10**:25
vulture, king **10**:26
vulture, lappet-faced **10**:27

W

wagtail, white **10**:28
wagtail, yellow **10**:29
wall lizard **5**:42
wall lizard, Italian **5**:35
warty (crested) newt **6**:44
wasteland grasshopper, blue-winged **4**:36
water buffalo **1**:44
water chevrotain **2**:22
water dragon, oriental **3**:25
water flea (daphnia) **3**:37
water measurer **6**:18
water pipit **7**:24
water vole, European **10**:23
wattled jacana **5**:22
waved whelk **10**:35
waxbill, red-cheeked (cordon-bleu) **10**:30
waxwing, cedar **10**:31
weaver, grenadier (red bishop) **10**:32
wels **10**:33
western tarsier **9**:35
whale, Baird's beaked **10**:34
whelk, waved **10**:35
whirligig beetle **1**:32
whiskered tern **9**:37
white, marbled **10**:36
white bat, Honduran **1**:24
white-cheeked gibbon **4**:29
white-eyed vireo **10**:21
white piranha **7**:25
white-sided dolphin, Pacific **3**:23
white stork **9**:25
white-tailed mongoose **6**:25
white wagtail **10**:28
whooper swan **9**:30
whydah, pin-tailed **10**:37
wild cat, European **2**:12
wild dog, African **3**:20
wild goat **4**:32
wolf, maned **10**:38
wood cockroach **2**:32
wood mouse **6**:39
wood sandpiper **8**:15
woolly spider monkey (muriqui) **6**:32
worm, horsehair **10**:39
worm, ice cream cone **10**:40
worm, peripatus velvet **10**:41
worm, red tube **10**:42

X-Y-Z

yellow-bellied glider **4**:31
yellow wagtail **10**:29
zebu **10**:44
zorilla (striped polecat) **7**:28